Apples Pears BOOK B

TEACHER'S NOTES

Third Edition

Hilary Burkard
& Tom Burkard

First published 2003, Hilary Burkard
Second Edition (Revised) 2006, Hilary Burkard
Third Edition (Revised) 2011, Hilary Burkard

ISBN: 978-1-905174-26-3

Tracing exercises produced using 'Handwriting For Windows'
available from: www.kber.co.uk

Published by Hilary Burkard

Distributed by
SOUND FOUNDATIONS
www.soundfoundations.co.uk
sales@soundfoundations.co.uk
☎08448 708158 FAX 08448 708172

Apples and Pears

The one stop programme for spelling, punctuation and grammar.
Ideal for group work and individual tutoring.

Getting started:

Which pupils will benefit from *Apples and Pears*?

Apples and Pears can be used with pupils of any age from 4 onward. It can be used with pupils of all abilities, including those with special needs. It can be used for one-on-one teaching, or it can be used with groups of pupils who are well-matched for ability. You should always use the placement tests to determine the appropriate starting point. Any pupil with a spelling age of less than 10 years will almost certainly benefit greatly from the programme.

Does it take any special training to use *Apples and Pears*?

Almost anyone with a bit of common sense can teach a child to spell with *Apples and Pears*. It is designed so that classroom assistants and parents can use it successfully, even with children who have reading problems. However, you must read these notes carefully. We are always happy to give advice by telephone or e-mail.

How does *Apples and Pears* work?

Apples and Pears is a direct instruction programme. The *Teacher's Notes* are scripts which tell the teacher what to say to the pupils. The pupils each have their own workbook. The constant interaction between teacher and pupil ensures a very high percentage of time-on-task, and it enables the teacher to correct mistakes immediately.

Why does *Apples and Pears* work?

Learning to write well puts a considerable load on a pupil's memory. If pupils do not have a firm grasp of spelling, punctuation and grammar, they will have less attention available for the content of their work. At least 35% of all pupils in Britain are very poor at spelling—poor enough for a spell checker to be of limited value.

Apples and Pears works on these principles:

1. Carefully planned structure ensures that material is taught in a logical order.
2. Every task is broken down into the smallest possible steps.
3. Continuous reinforcement ensures that no time is wasted by teaching skills that are eventually forgotten.
4. Pupils are trained to hear each sound in a word—this greatly reduces memory load required to learn to spell.

5. Memory load is drastically reduced by a 'morphemic' strategy—pupils learn interchangeable building blocks in words. Each morpheme* in the word "ex-cept-ion-al-ly" can be used in dozens, if not hundreds, of other words. They also learn the rules for **dropping the 'e'** (hoping, hopeless); **doubling** (fitting, fitness) and **changing the 'y' to 'i'** (studied, studying).*
6. Irregular words are introduced at a controlled rate. Pupils with learning difficulties find these the most difficult to master.
7. Extensive dictation exercises give pupils an understanding of correct sentence structure and punctuation, and assists transfer of skills to other written work.
8. Multi-sensory techniques work with all pupils, regardless as to their individual strengths and weaknesses.

How often should I use *Apples and Pears*?
Ideally, you should use it every school day. With special needs pupils, this is all but essential. With other pupils, three lessons per week is the minimum. Each lesson will take about 10 to 20 minutes, depending upon the skill of the pupils and the experience of the teacher.

The Teacher's Notes:
At first glance, these may seem a bit daunting, but they all follow fairly standard patterns. Once you get used to them, you will only need to glance at them occasionally. You do not have to follow them word-for-word, and you should adapt the notes to your own style. **There are three golden rules:**

1. **Keep your eyes on your pupils and their workbooks.** If necessary, use a sheet of paper so you don't lose your place in the Teacher's Notes.
2. **Correct all mistakes immediately, if not sooner.**
3. **Keep the pace cracking along.** Don't let pupils distract you—the others will get bored and lose the thread.

Correcting errors:
The best way to correct an error is to spell the word orally as the pupil writes down the letters. Then have the pupil cover the work and spell it orally, or write it (whichever is easiest).

---

* A morpheme is the smallest unit of a word that has a meaning. e.g., the morphemes in 'watering' are *water + ing*, but its syllables are wah'ter ing.

Apples and Pears

When teaching groups, it is usually best to ask a pupil who has spelled the word correctly to spell it aloud, while others correct their work. When correcting their work, pupils should rewrite the whole word, not modify odd letters.

Reviewing problem spellings: individual tutoring
Each time the pupil makes a mistake and is unable to self-correct immediately, underline the word in your Teacher's Notes, and use the correction procedure outlined above. At the end of the lesson—and at the beginning of the next lesson—use the following procedure:

1. Make a list of the problem words. Spell each one out loud, and have the pupil write them down (on a white board or a blank sheet of paper), reading what they have just written.

   Example: *Teacher: "Write b-r-o-w-n....what word?"*
   Pupil: "brown"

2. Ask the pupil to look at each word, and point to each letter and spell it out loud.

   Example: *Teacher: "Spell the word brown. Point to each letter as you say it."*
   Pupil: "b-r-o-w-n"

3. Cover the work, and dictate each word as the pupil writes it from memory. Intervene and correct as soon as the pupil makes a mistake.

4. Covert the work, and ask the pupil to spell each word out loud from memory.

With special needs pupils, you should not do more than 3 or 4 words at a time. If you have more words on your list, do it in two goes. Otherwise, they may forget the spellings and make errors. The whole point of this exercise to make sure they **don't** make mistakes.

With very young pupils who have not learned letter names, it will be necessary for them to use letter sounds when spelling orally.

How fast should I go?
Most pupils can do a level each day with very little trouble. However, dyslexic pupils may need to go slower—perhaps half a level a day. **But if a pupil is not getting at least 90% of his spellings right, you are going too fast.**

Apples and Pears

Mastery Tests:
If a pupil fails a Mastery Test, you **must** go back. Do not give the pupil the benefit of the doubt in borderline cases. Otherwise, your pupil will keep making more and more mistakes, and this will destroy confidence and enthusiasm. Children seldom mind having to repeat material—usually, they are relieved to be working at the appropriate level.

Teaching groups:
Teaching groups is a far more efficient use of a teacher's time, and it is more fun. Competitions will keep your pupils keenly engaged. Always have all the pupils seated facing you—you cannot teach the back of a child's head. Ideally, you want to be able to see every worksheet without having to move more than a few steps. Do not be afraid to mix children from different years. Do not include children who are slow writers—the rest of the group will get bored waiting for them.

Saturday, 27 October 2018

*(At the beginning of each lesson, write the day and date on the white board. For instance, write **Wednesday, 5 January 2011.***)*

At the beginning of each lesson, you will copy the day and date into your workbook. Write the day and the date in your workbook.

1. **Key sentence:**

   *(On the first line the sentence is partially written in boxes—one box for each **sound**. The pupil traces the sentence, filling in the empty boxes as he goes. Make sure he starts with a capital letter, has the right groups or individual letters in each box and finishes with a full stop. The pupil then copies the sentence onto line 2, check spelling and punctuation. Cover the work and dictate the sentence, if the pupil gets stuck or makes a mistake, show him the original.)*

   The sentence should say *'We saw who came over.'*

   Trace the sentence, filling in the blanks.

   Copy the sentence onto line 2.

   Now cover up the sentence and write it from dictation on line 3.

2. **Spelling patterns:**

   (New spelling patterns are introduced and tricky spellings reviewed in this exercise. Make sure the pupil has copied correctly before covering and dictating. As with the Key Sentence; show him the original if he forgets the spelling.)

   Read the words in Part 2. *(Prompt if necessary.)*

   Copy them onto line 2.

   Now cover your work and write them from dictation on line 3.

moon	*shoot*	*broom*
pool	*choose*	*smooth*

* Make this standard procedure for all written work. This is a simple and virtually fool-proof method of teaching children to spell the days and months. It is also essential training for writing formal letters.

3. **Word sums:**

(This exercise introduces the morphemic principle in spelling. Pupils learn to spell the building blocks of more complex words and to join them together.)

Review morphemes *'mis', 'er'* and *'ing'*.

Add these morphemes together:

longer	*lighted*	*misspelled*
blinker	*boxer*	*misleading*

Read the words you have written.

Now turn the page and write the words from dictation.

(Dictate the words.)

4. **Filling in the blanks:**

(The worksheet has a blank for each missing sound. Dictate each word and make sure the pupil traces the word and fills in each blank correctly as he goes.)

Trace the words, filling in the blanks.

put	*brass*	*wonder*
going	*bowler*	*knowing*

5. **Morpheme analysis:**

*(The reciprocal of **Word Sums**. Pupils learn to identify the morphemes in words and to separate them.)*

Fill in the blanks to show the morphemes in each word.

cook + er	*real + ly*	*de + press + ing*
mend + ed	*kiss + ing*	*heat + er*

6. **Writing words:**

*(This exercise recycles the words practised in **Filling in the Blanks**. This time the pupil writes the words from dictation.)*

put	*brass*	*wonder*
going	*bowler*	*knowing*

7. **Introduction to commas:**

I will read the first sentence in part 7.

If you would like to go now, please stand up.

The little mark between the words *'now'* and *'please'* is called a comma.

- What do we call this mark? **(A comma.)**

We can use a comma to show a short pause in speech. I will read the sentence again and you will hear a little pause between *'now'* and *'please'*.

If you would like to go now, please stand up.

Now I will read the second sentence:

Should we have lunch now, or would you like a drink?

I want you to put the comma in the correct place.
Now I will read the sentence again, and you decide where to put the comma.

Should we have lunch now, or would you like a drink?
(Exaggerate the pause slightly and correct if necessary)

8. **Spelling test:**

(Dictate each word. If the pupil is confused by homophones such as be/bee, put the word in context.)

mean	*bosses*	*some*	*done*	*fix*
father	*about*	*your*	*clean*	*better*

9. Sentence dictation:

(Try to get the pupil to remember the whole sentence before he starts writing, as this will help to improve his memory. If he can't, dictate it in chunks—avoid dictating one word at a time.
*The **Spelling Test** and **Sentence Dictation** should always be done at one sitting, if at all possible, as the spelling test rehearses words used in the dictation, which may be forgotten by the next day.)*

1. *When your father mended our car, he forgot to fix the heater.*
2. *When my lunch is done, would you please clean out the cooker.*
3. *Some bosses are really mean, and they make you cross.*
4. *The less said about those misspellings, the better.*

All of those sentences have commas.
I will read the sentences again, you decide where the commas should go. *(Exaggerate the pause slightly.)*

10. Word Bingo:

(Although this game is designed for a group of pupils, it is always enjoyed in one-to-one lessons—not least because the pupil always wins.
Dictate the words to the pupils, who can write them in any square of the grid. Then, call out the words in a different order and nominate a different pupil to spell each word. Pupils cross off each word they have spelled correctly. The winner is the first pupil with four crosses in a row.)

lay	*pray*	*remark*	*farmer*
refill	*partly*	*cooking*	*howling*
wants	*bring*	*today*	*drink*
quiz	*what*	*have*	*hay*

Apples and Pears Level 2:

(Write the day and the date on the white board.)
Copy the day and the date into your workbook.

1. **Key sentence:**
   The sentence should say *'We saw who came over.'*
   Trace the sentence, filling in the blanks.
   Copy the sentence onto line 2.
   Now cover up the sentence and write it from dictation on line 3.

2. Spelling patterns:
   Read the words in Part 2. *(Prompt if necessary.)*
   Copy them onto line 2.
   Now cover your work and write them from dictation on line 3.

oat	*boat*	*coat*
load	*road*	*soap*

3. **Word sums:**
   Review morphemes *'re'*, *'less'* and *'ing'*.
   Add these morphemes together:

endless	*crossing*	*repress*
missing	*classless*	*rebrand*

   Read the words you have written.
   Now cover your work and write the words from dictation.

4. **Filling in the blanks:**
   Trace the words, filling in the blanks.

please	*wrong*	*choose*
fear	*meal*	*smooth*

5. Morpheme analysis:
Fill in the blanks to show the morphemes in each word.

fix + ed	*slight + ly*	*real + ly*
re + serve	*reach + es*	*sight + less*

6. Writing words:

please	*wrong*	*choose*
fear	*meal*	*smooth*

7. Spelling test:

away	*done*	*clean*	*maybe*	*shoot*
when	*least*	*would*	*some*	*broom*

8. Sentence dictation:
Every sentence must begin with a capital letter.
- What should every sentence begin with? **(A capital letter)**

(Repeat until firm)
Every sentence must end with a full stop* or a question mark.
- What do you put at the end of a sentence?
  (A full stop or a question mark†) *(Repeat until firm)*

1. *Would you please put your broom away?*
- Is this sentence asking or telling? **(Asking)**
- What do you put at the end of this sentence? **(A question mark)**

2. *My father knows how to shoot pool.*
- Is this sentence asking or telling? **(Telling)**
- What do you put at the end of this sentence? **(A full stop)**

3. *At least you can clean out your room tonight.*
- Is this sentence asking or telling? **(Telling)**
- What do you put at the end of this sentence? **(A full stop)**

---

* USA: full stop=period
† Exclamation marks are overused in children's writing, and should not be encouraged.

8. Continued:

4. When your sister is done, she will make some tea.

- Is this sentence asking or telling? **(Telling)**
- What do you put at the end of this sentence? **(A full stop)**

Sentence 4 should have a comma. I will read the sentence again, and you decide where to put the comma.

(Exaggerate the pause slightly.)

9. Crossword:

(Pupils should read the words in the puzzle before they start. Imposing a time limit prevents the pupil using it to waste time.)

Read the words before you start.

Apples and Pears Level 3:

(Write the day and the date on the white board.)
Copy the day and the date into your workbook.

1. **Key sentence:**
   The sentence should say *'We saw who came over.'*
   Trace the sentence, filling in the blanks.
   Copy the sentence onto line 2.
   Now cover up the sentence and write it from dictation on line 3.

2. **Spelling patterns:**
   Read the words in Part 2. *(Prompt if necessary.)*
   Copy them onto line 2.
   Now cover your work and write them from dictation on line 3.

ladder	*paper*	*bigger*
rather	*danger*	*gather*

3. **Word sums:**
   Review morphemes *'de'*, *'es'* and *'ly'*.
   Add these morphemes together:

teaches	*delight*	*smoothly*
deport	*cleanly*	*classes*

   Read the words you have written.
   Now turn the page and write the words from dictation.

4. **Filling in the blanks:**
   Trace the words, filling in the blanks.

some	*howl*	*soap*
shove	*bliss*	*road*

5. Morpheme analysis:
Fill in the blanks to show the morphemes in each word.

load + er	*pass + es*	*box + ed*
speak + er	*year + ly*	*dress + ing*

6. Writing words:

some	*howl*	*soap*
shove	*bliss*	*road*

7. Spelling test:

boat	*strong*	*boss*	*make*	*quickly*
box	*like*	*leave*	*when*	*delighted*

8. Sentence dictation:
Every sentence must begin with a capital letter.
- What should every sentence begin with? **(A capital letter)**

(Repeat until firm)
Every sentence must end with a full stop or a question mark.
- What do you put at the end of a sentence? **(A full stop or a question mark)**

1. *Please tell me when you are done mending her boat.*
- Is this sentence asking or telling? **(Telling)**
- What do you put at the end of this sentence? **(A full stop)**

2. *Would your boss like to give us a hand?*
- Is this sentence asking or telling? **(Asking)**
- What do you put at the end of this sentence? **(A question mark)**

3. *I would be delighted to make a strong box.*
- Is this sentence asking or telling? **(Telling)**
- What do you put at the end of this sentence? **(A full stop)**

8. Continued:

4. I will help you put on your coat, and then we can leave quickly.

- Is this sentence asking or telling? **(Telling)**
- What do you put at the end of this sentence? **(A full stop)**

Sentence 4 should have a comma. I will read the sentence again, and you decide where to put the comma.
(Exaggerate the pause slightly.)

9. Word search:
Read the words before you start.

Apples and Pears Level 4:

(Write the day and the date on the white board.)
Copy the day and the date into your workbook.

1. **Key sentence:**
   The sentence should say *'We saw who came over.'*
   Trace the sentence, filling in the blanks.
   Copy the sentence onto line 2.
   Now cover up the sentence and write it from dictation on line 3.

2. **Spelling patterns:**
   Read the words in Part 2. *(Prompt if necessary.)*
   Copy them onto line 2.
   Now cover your work and write them from dictation on line 3.

soft	*left*	*lift*
gift	*raft*	*drift*

3. **Word sums:**
   New morpheme *'un'.*
   Add these morphemes together:

unload	*unseat*	*unless*
unclean	*undress*	*unreal*

   Read the words you have written.
   Now cover your work and write the words from dictation.

4. **Filling in the blanks:**
   Trace the words, filling in the blanks.

make	*done*	*shook*
some	*above*	*when*

5. Morpheme analysis:
Fill in the blanks to show the morphemes in each word.

mis + lay	*cross + ed*	*spend + er*
like + ly	*kiss + ing*	*smooth + er*

6. Writing words:

make	*done*	*shook*
some	*above*	*when*

7. Spelling test:

coat	*bigger*	*read*	*hall*	*danger*
rather	*grass*	*load*	*better*	*paper*

8. Sentence dictation:
Every sentence must begin with a capital letter.

- What should every sentence begin with? **(A capital letter)**

(Repeat until firm)
Every sentence must end with a full stop or a question mark.

- What do you put at the end of a sentence?
  (A full stop or a question mark)

1. *We will be out of danger if we stand on the grass.*
2. *I would rather sit down and read the paper.*
3. *It would be better if you gave him a bigger load.*
4. *Put your coat on the stand in the hall, please.*

Sentence 4 should have a comma. I will read the sentence again, and you decide where to put the comma. *(Exaggerate the pause slightly.)*

9. Crossword:
Read the words before you start.

(Write the day and the date on the white board.)
Copy the day and the date into your workbook.

1. **Words beginning with 'k':**
   Find part 1 in your workbook.
   Listen carefully—this is a new rule. If a word starts with the sound /*c*/, use the letter *'k'* when the next letter is *'e'* or *'i'*.
   - If a word begins with the sound /*c*/, when do you use the letter *'k'*?

   (When the next letter is 'e' or 'i'.) *(Repeat until letter-perfect.)*

2. **Spelling patterns:**
   Read the words in Part 2. *(Prompt if necessary.)*
   Copy them onto line 2.
   Now cover your work and write them from dictation on line 3.

keep	*kiss*	*keg*
kit	*kill*	*Ken*
kind	*kid*	*kept*
king	*kick*	*kitchen*

3. **The vowel letters:**
   The vowel letters are *a, e, i, o* and *u*.
   Circle all the vowel letters on lines 1 and 2.
   Turn the page, now circle all the vowel letters on lines 3 and 4.

4. **Sentence dictation:**
   All names and titles begin with a capital letter.
   - What do all names and titles begin with? **(A capital letter)**

   1. *I would never kiss a cat.*

   - Is there a name or title in this sentence? **(No)**

   2. *The King gave our kid a kiss.*

   - Is there a name or title in this sentence? **(The King)**
   - What should *'King'* begin with? **(A capital letter)**

4. Continued.

3. *Keep on kicking the ball.*
- Is there a name or title in this sentence? **(No)**

4. *We were kept behind after class.*
- Is there a name or title in this sentence? **(No)**

5. *Ken kept a keg of beer in his kitchen.*
- Is there a name or title in this sentence? **(Ken)**
- What should *'Ken'* begin with? **(A capital letter)**

5. Morphemes:

A morpheme is the smallest part of a word that has meaning.
- What do we call the smallest part of a word that has meaning? **(A morpheme)**
- What is the first morpheme in *reporting*? **(re)**
- What is the next morpheme? **(port)**
- What is the next morpheme? **(ing)**

Now we will do some oral drills.
- What is the first morpheme in *slicer*? **(slice)**
- What is the next morpheme? **(er)**.

(Repeat for the following words:)

relaxing = re + lax + ing

hurrying = hurry + ing

powerful = power + ful

helper = help + er

delightful = de + light + ful

unrewarding = un + re + ward + ing

uselessly = use + less + ly

(Write the day and the date on the white board.)
Copy the day and the date into your workbook.

1. **Key sentence review:**
   Write the following sentences:

   1. *Can she see me?*
   2. *I have all of the cards.*
   3. *I want to come down now.*

2. **Spelling patterns:**
   You are going to write words spelled with *'ve', 'ow', 'all'* and *'y'*. When I say each word, point to the spelling pattern you will use and then write the word.

save	*town*	*ball*	*love*
try	*power*	*wall*	*shy*
dry	*small*	*above*	*growl*

3. **Word sum dictation:**
   A morpheme is the smallest part of a word that has meaning.
   - What do we call the smallest part of a word that has meaning? **(A morpheme)**
   - What is the first morpheme in *spying*? **(spy)**

   Write *spy* in the first blank in part 3.
   - What is the next morpheme in *spying*? **(ing)**

   Write *ing* in the next blank.
   Now write *spying* in the third blank.
   (Repeat for the following words:)

small + er = smaller	*brave + ly = bravely*
howl + ed = howled	*re + call = recall*
call + ing = calling	*clown + ing = clowning*
call + er = caller	

3. Continued.

Now turn the page and write these words from dictation.

spying	*smaller*	*bravely*	*howled*
recall	*calling*	*clowning*	*caller*

4. Copying the letters in words:

I'll spell some words and you write them down.
Then tell me what words I spelled.

brave	*crown*	*stall*
shove	*sky*	*better*

Now cover your work and write these words again on the lines below. *(Dictate the words.)*

5. Word search:

Read the words before you start.

6. Spelling test:

has	*luck*	*why*	*gave*	*sharp*
they	*was*	*won*	*sweeper*	*form*
have	*come*	*how*	*much*	*queen*
do	*what*	*her*	*shell*	*of*
want	*drill*	*to*	*book*	*little*

7. Word sums: *(Optional)*

Make at least eight real words from the following morphemes.
(Teacher may suggest words if necessary.)

de- *re-* *port* *part* *press* *-ing* *-ed*

Apples and Pears Level 7:

(Write the day and the date on the white board.)
Copy the day and the date into your workbook.

1. **Key sentence:**
   The sentence should say
   'There is nothing on the table for dinner.'
   Trace the sentence, filling in the blanks.
   Copy the sentence onto line 2.
   Now cover up the sentence and write it from dictation on line 3.

2. **Spelling patterns:**
   Read the words in Part 2. *(Prompt if necessary.)*
   Copy them onto line 2.
   Now cover your work and write them from dictation on line 3.

goat	*float*	*roam*
toad	*loan*	*oat*

3. **Word sums:**
   Review morphemes *'ed'*, *'er'*, and *'mis'*.
   Add these morphemes together:

loaded	*gifted*	*smoother*
mistook	*misplay*	*drifter*

   Read the words you have written.
   Now cover your work and write the words from dictation.

4. **Filling in the blanks:**
   Trace the words, filling in the blanks.

rather	*our*	*soap*	*kill*
shrunk	*strong*	*quiz*	*kept*

5. **Morpheme analysis:**
   Fill in the blanks to show the morphemes in each word.

mis + spend	*glass + es*	*cross + ly*
hand + ed	*re + load*	*gather + ed*

6. Writing words:

rather	*our*	*soap*	*kill*
shrunk	*strong*	*quiz*	*kept*

7. Spelling test:

came	*pond*	*they*	*speaking*	*left*
ladder	*drifted*	*paper*	*out*	*raft*

8. Sentence dictation:

All names and titles begin with a capital letter.

- What do all names and titles begin with? **(A capital letter)**

1. Who left the paper over by the ladder?

- Is there a name or title in this sentence? **(No)**

2. They saw who came down the road with Queen Bess.

- Is there a name or title in this sentence? **(Queen Bess)**
- What should *'Queen'* begin with? **(A capital letter)**
- What should *'Bess'* begin with? **(A capital letter)**

3. When you are done speaking, put on your coat.

- Is there a name or title in this sentence? **(No)**

4. Our raft drifted out on the pond, and Miss Clay had to come and get us.

- Is there a name or title in this sentence? **(Miss Clay)**
- What should *'Miss'* begin with? **(A capital letter)**
- What should *'Clay'* begin with? **(A capital letter)**

Sentences 3 and 4 should each have a comma. I will read the sentences again, and you decide where to put the commas.
(Exaggerate the pause slightly.)

9. Crossword:

Read the words before you start.

Apples and Pears Level 8:

(Write the day and the date on the white board.)
Copy the day and the date into your workbook.

1. **Key sentence:**
   The sentence should say *'There is nothing on the table for dinner.'*
   Trace the sentence, filling in the blanks.
   Copy the sentence onto line 2.
   Now cover up the sentence and write it from dictation on line 3.

2. **Spelling patterns:**
   Read the words in Part 2. *(Prompt if necessary.)*
   Copy them onto line 2.
   Now cover your work and write them from dictation on line 3.

wall	*walk*	*tall*
talk	*ball*	*bald*

3. **Word sums:**
   Review morphemes *'re', 'un', 'less'.*
   Add these morphemes together:

paperless	*unload*	*unclear*
reloan	*thankless*	*refloat*

   Read the words you have written.
   Now turn the page and write the words from dictation.

4. **Filling in the blanks:**
   Trace the words, filling in the blanks.

came	*better*	*bright*	*kid*
saw	*sister*	*who*	*keg*

5. Morpheme analysis:
Fill in the blanks to show the morphemes in each word.

year + ly	*loan + ed*	*mother + less*
miss + es	*tall + er*	*swing + ing*

6. Writing words:

came	*better*	*bright*	*kid*
saw	*sister*	*who*	*keg*

7. Spelling test:

some	*oak*	*what*	*smooth*	*loaned*
little	*those*	*paper*	*mother*	*wants*

8. Sentence dictation:
All names and titles begin with a capital letter.
- What do all names and titles begin with? **(A capital letter)**

1. *What are those boys doing over by the oak tree?*
- Is there a name or title in this sentence? **(No)**

2. *My father said that he loaned Lord North some paper.*
- Is there a name or title in this sentence? **(Lord North)**
- What should *'Lord'* begin with? **(A capital letter)**
- What should *'North'* begin with? **(A capital letter)**

3. *When my mother left, she was a little put out.*
- Is there a name or title in this sentence? **(No)**

4. *King Roy wants a coat that is soft and smooth.*
- Is there a name or title in this sentence? **(King Roy)**
- What should *'King'* begin with? **(A capital letter)**
- What should *'Roy'* begin with? **(A capital letter)**

Sentence 3 should have a comma. I will read the sentence again, and you decide where to put the comma.
(Exaggerate the pause slightly.)

9. Word bingo:

(See page 10 for instructions)

seat	*teach*	*real*	*fighter*
howling	*trusted*	*bowler*	*string*
shout	*belt*	*sharply*	*likely*
reserve	*started*	*still*	*think*

Apples and Pears Level 9:

(Write the day and the date on the white board.)

Copy the day and the date into your workbook.

1. **Key sentence:**
   The sentence should say *'There is nothing on the table for dinner.'*
   Trace the sentence, filling in the blanks.
   Copy the sentence onto line 2.
   Now cover up the sentence and write it from dictation on line 3.

2. **Spelling patterns:**
   Read the words in Part 2. *(Prompt if necessary.)*
   Copy them onto line 2.
   Now cover your work and write them from dictation on line 3.

cattle	*middle*	*jungle*
rifle	*marble*	*trouble*

3. **Word sums:**
   Review morphemes *'de', 'es', 'ly'.*
   Add these morphemes together:

delay	*boxes*	*coolly*
misses	*softly*	*deserve*

   Read the words you have written.
   Now cover your work and write the words from dictation.

4. **Filling in the blanks:**
   Trace the words, filling in the blanks.

could	*why*	*wonder*
quack	*should*	*were*

5. Morpheme analysis:
Fill in the blanks to show the morphemes in each word.

gift + ed	*smooth + er*	*roam + ing*
soap + ed	*soft + ly*	*walk + ed*

6. Writing words:

could	*why*	*wonder*
quack	*should*	*were*

7. Spelling test:

bald	*goat*	*what*	*could*	*bigger*
talking	*leader*	*teacher*	*were*	*walk*

8. Sentence dictation:
All names and titles begin with a capital letter.

- What do all names and titles begin with? **(A capital letter)**

1. *Our goat is bigger than your little toad.*
2. *When those bald men came in, they saw what Miss Little was doing.*
3. *Could you walk over there and talk to our leader, please?*
4. *Could you see who was talking to our teacher?*

Sentences 2 and 3 should each have a comma. I will read the sentences again, and you decide where to put the commas. *(Exaggerate the pause slightly.)*

9. Crossword:
Read the words before you start.

Sentence dictation:

(These sentences will provide additional review and reinforcement. Many pupils will find it tiring to write all twelve sentences in one go, so here are some suggestions:

1. *If you are working one-to-one, you can try our points system.*
   We award one point for remembering capitals and full stops, one point for remembering the words in the sentence without continual prompts, one point for neat handwriting, two points for no spelling errors, or one point for only one spelling error. Once they have earned 24 points, they are finished with the exercise.

2. *Working with groups, we often pit the boys against the girls, and see which group makes the fewest mistakes. You can vary this with individual competitions, and you can give special prizes for neat handwriting.*

   You will no doubt think of other ideas—if you come up with any good ones, let us know!)

Every sentence must end with a full stop or a question mark.
- What do you put at the end of a sentence?
  (A full stop or a question mark)

All names and titles begin with a capital letter.
- What do all names and titles begin with? **(A capital letter)**

1. *The hunter lost his rifle in the middle of the jungle.*
2. *Would you make some toast for dinner, please?*
3. *Could Ken walk over there and talk to my father?*
4. *Who wants to come out for a trip in my little boat?*
5. *I know what those smooth talking dealers are like.*
6. *Gather up your coats quickly when you are done looking.*
7. *Why are all those boys playing out in the road?*
8. *How was Miss Black going to get away last night?*
9. *Lord North came in and saw what the speaker was saying.*

10. *The toothless old man said that he wanted a drink.*

11. *I would rather not choose what sort of coat to put on.*

12. *Our team won the toss, so we can choose to kick off.*

Placement / Mastery Test:

Test to be used after Level 10:

(See the instructions for Mastery Tests on page 6.)

gift	*smooth*	*rather*	*loaded*	*walk*
really	*middle*	*fighter*	*motherly*	*delay*
reserve	*left*	*pool*	*paper*	*soap*
king	*shrinking*	*who*	*loan*	*trouble*

Scoring:

Mastery:	*0-2 errors—*	*pass*
	3-4 errors—	*review spelling patterns and retest the following day.*
	5+ errors—	*go back to Level 1.*
Placement:	*0-2 errors—*	*pass; start at this level, or go on to the next placement test*
	2+ errors—	*go back to the placement test at the end of Book A.*

(At the beginning of every lesson write the day and the date on the white board —be sure to do this every day.)

Copy the day and the date into your workbook.

1. **Key sentence review:**

   Write the following sentences:

   1. *I will sell the car.*
   2. *Why was he doing that?*
   3. *What are those boys doing?*

2. **Spelling patterns:**

   You are going to write words spelled with *'oo', 'ay'* and *'ink'*. When I say each word, point to the spelling pattern you will use and then write the word.

stink	*away*	*shook*	*clay*
stay	*good*	*blink*	*foot*
think	*wood*	*pray*	*slink*

3. **Word sum dictation:**

   (This exercise introduces the morphemic principle in spelling. Pupils learn to spell the building blocks of more complex words and to join them together.)

   A morpheme is the smallest part of a word that has meaning.

   - What do we call the smallest part of a word that has meaning? **(A morpheme)**
   - What is the first morpheme in *motherly*? **(mother)**

   Write *mother* in the first blank in part 3.

   - What is the next morpheme in *motherly*? **(ly)**

   Write *ly* in the next blank.

   Now write *motherly* in the third blank.

3. Continued.

(Repeat for the following words:)

re + serve = reserve	*tight + er = tighter*
tax + es = taxes	*un + clear = unclear*
de + lay = delay	*fear + less = fearless*
mis + spell = misspell	

Now turn the page and write these words from dictation.
(Dictate the words)

motherly	*reserve*	*tighter*	*taxes*
unclear	*delay*	*fearless*	*misspell*

4. Copying the letters in words:

I'll spell some words and you write them down.
Then tell me what words I spelled.

took	*brink*	*away*
slink	*wood*	*day*

Now cover your work and write these words again on the lines below. *(Dictate the words.)*

5. Word search:

(Pupils should read the words in the puzzle before they start. Imposing a time limit prevents the pupil using it to waste time.)

Read the words before you start.

6. Spelling test:

(Dictate each word. If the pupil is confused by homophones such as be/bee, put the word in context.)

were	*so*	*would*	*father*	*some*
how	*what*	*those*	*come*	*bowl*
be	*could*	*won*	*said*	*sharper*
want	*heater*	*thinking*	*dealer*	*needless*
they	*slightly*	*reborn*	*coated*	*wrongly*

7. Word sums: *(Optional)*

Make at least eight real words from the following morphemes.

(Teacher may suggest words if necessary.)

un- *re-* *born* *seat* *real* *-ed* *-ly*

(Write the day and the date on the white board—be sure to do this every day.)
Copy the day and the date into your workbook.

1. **Key sentence:**
   *(On the first line the sentence is partially written in boxes—one box for each **sound**. The pupil traces the sentence, filling in the empty boxes as he goes. Make sure he starts with a capital letter, has the right groups or individual letters in each box and finishes with a question mark. The pupil then copies the sentence onto line 2, check spelling and punctuation. Cover the work and dictate the sentence, if the pupil gets stuck or makes a mistake, show him the original.)*
   The sentence should say *'Many of these girls come from England.'*
   Trace the sentence, filling in the blanks.
   Copy the sentence onto line 2.
   Now cover up the sentence and write it from dictation on line 3.

2. **Spelling patterns:**
   (New spelling patterns are introduced and tricky spellings reviewed in this exercise. Make sure the pupil has copied correctly before covering and dictating. As with the Key Sentence, show him the original if he forgets the spelling.)
   Read the words in Part 2. *(Prompt if necessary.)*
   Copy them onto line 2.
   Now cover your work and write them from dictation on line 3.

bank	*sank*	*tank*
drank	*thank*	*blank*

3. Word sums:

(This exercise introduces the morphemic principle in spelling. Pupils learn to spell the building blocks of more complex words and to join them together.)

New morpheme *'ful'.*

Add these morphemes together:

wishful	*harmful*	*powerful*
helpful	*playful*	*bashful*

Read the words you have written.

Now cover your work and write the words from dictation.

4. Filling in the blanks:

(The worksheet has a blank for each missing sound. Dictate each word and make sure the pupil traces the word and fills in each blank correctly as he goes.)

Trace the words, filling in the blanks.

who	*came*	*table*
saw	*cattle*	*dinner*

5. Morpheme analysis:

Fill in the blanks to show the morphemes in each word.

talk + ed	*drift + ed*	*float + ing*
shoot + er	*mean + ing*	*clean + ly*

6. Writing words:

(This exercise recycles the words practised in ***Filling in the Blanks****. This time the pupil writes the words from dictation.)*

who	*came*	*table*
saw	*cattle*	*dinner*

7. Spelling test:

past	*danger*	*were*	*rifle*	*tonight*
nothing	*shoot*	*they*	*raft*	*middle*

8. Sentence dictation:

1. *Could you shoot your rifle over there?*
2. *If you walk down the middle of the road, you will be in danger.*
3. *They were floating past us on the raft.*
4. *There is nothing left to eat tonight.*

Sentence 2 should have a comma. I will read the sentence again, you decide where the comma should go.
(Read the sentence ***without*** *exaggerating the pause.)*

9. Word bingo:
(Although this game is designed for a group of pupils, it is always enjoyed in one-to-one lessons—not least because the pupil always wins.
Dictate the words to the pupils, who can write them in any square of the grid. Then, call out the words in a different order and nominate a different pupil to spell each word. Pupils cross off each word they have spelled correctly. The winner is the first pupil with four crosses in a row.)

mess	*press*	*miss*	*dishes*
boxes	*going*	*quickly*	*father*
know	*road*	*wrong*	*wishes*
kisses	*down*	*were*	*sorted*

Apples and Pears Level 13:

(Write the day and the date on the white board—be sure to do this every day.)
Copy the day and the date into your workbook.

1. **Key sentence:**
   The sentence should say *'Many of these girls come from England.'*
   Trace the sentence, filling in the blanks.
   Copy the sentence onto line 2.
   Now cover up the sentence and write it from dictation on line 3.

2. **Spelling patterns:**
   Read the words in Part 2. *(Prompt if necessary.)*
   Copy them onto line 2.
   Now cover your work and write them from dictation on line 3.

summer	*ruler*	*butter*
silver	*rubber*	*super*

3. **Word sums:**
   Review morphemes *'ed', 'er'* and *'mis'*.
   Add these morphemes together:

thanked	*talker*	*mismark*
loader	*misfit*	*reached*

   Read the words you have written.
   Now turn the page and write the words from dictation.

4. **Filling in the blanks:**
   Trace the words, filling in the blanks.

make	*when*	*marble*	*real*
came	*danger*	*wrong*	*kick*

5. Morpheme analysis:
Fill in the blanks to show the morphemes in each word.

saw + ing	*love + ly*	*lay + ing*
harm + less	*de + lay*	*roam + ing*

6. Writing words:

make	*when*	*marble*	*real*
came	*danger*	*wrong*	*kick*

7. Spelling test:

nothing	*meal*	*mother*	*many*	*goats*
thank	*table*	*dinner*	*jungle*	*done*

8. Sentence dictation:
Every sentence must begin with a capital letter.
- What should every sentence begin with? **(A capital letter)**

(Repeat until firm)
Every sentence must end with a full stop or a question mark.
- What do you put at the end of a sentence?

(A full stop or a question mark)

1. *Please thank your mother for the lovely dinner.*
- Is this sentence asking or telling? **(Telling)**
- What do you put at the end of this sentence? **(A full stop)**

2. *There are many goats roaming in the jungle.*
- Is this sentence asking or telling? **(Telling)**
- What do you put at the end of this sentence? **(A full stop)**

3. *Who left this meal on the table?*
- Is this sentence asking or telling? **(Asking)**
- What do you put at the end of this sentence? **(A question mark)**

8. Continued.

4. *Now that we are done, we have nothing to talk over.*

- Is this sentence asking or telling? **(Telling)**
- What do you put at the end of this sentence? **(A full stop)**

Sentence 4 should have a comma. I will read the sentence again, you decide where the comma should go.
*(Read the sentence **without** exaggerating the pause.)*

9. Crossword:
Read the words before you start.

1. **Key sentence:**
   The sentence should say *'Many of these girls come from England.'*
   Trace the sentence, filling in the blanks.
   Copy the sentence onto line 2.
   Now cover up the sentence and write it from dictation on line 3.

2. **Spelling patterns:**
   Read the words in Part 2. *(Prompt if necessary.)*
   Copy them onto line 2.
   Now cover your work and write them from dictation on line 3.

fell	*felt*	*bell*
belt	*well*	*weld*

3. **Word sums:**
   Review morphemes *'ful'*, *'re'* and *'un'*.
   Add these morphemes together:

powerful	*undress*	*unclear*
refloat	*thankful*	*repress*

   Read the words you have written.
   Now cover your work and write the words from dictation.

4. **Filling in the blanks:**
   Trace the words, filling in the blanks.

they	*would*	*know*
nothing	*were*	*bald*

5.Morpheme analysis:
   Fill in the blanks to show the morphemes in each word.

loan + ing	*class + less*	*brand + ed*
kiss + ing	*wrong + ly*	*mis + spend*

6. Writing words:

they	*would*	*know*
nothing	*were*	*bald*

7. Spelling test:

paper	*some*	*trouble*	*rubber*	*oak*
thank	*butter*	*put*	*soft*	*table*

8. Sentence dictation:

All names and titles begin with a capital letter.

- What do all names and titles begin with? **(A capital letter)**

1. *Thank you for loaning me a rubber and some paper.*
- Is there a name or title in this sentence? **(No)**

2. *How did King Roy know that they were in deep trouble?*
- Is there a name or title in this sentence? **(King Roy)**
- What should 'King' begin with? **(A capital letter)**
- What should 'Roy' begin with? **(A capital letter)**

3. *Did Miss Silver come over for dinner last night?*
- Is there a name or title in this sentence? **(Miss Silver)**
- What should 'Miss' begin with? **(A capital letter)**
- What should 'Silver' begin with? **(A capital letter)**

4. *Put the soft butter on the table, please.*
- Is there a name or title in this sentence? **(No)**

Sentence 4 should have a comma. I will read the sentence again, and you decide where to put the comma.
(Read the sentence ***without*** *exaggerating the pause.)*

9. Word search:

Read the words before you start.

Apples and Pears Level 15:

(Write the day and the date on the white board—be sure to do this every day.)
Copy the day and the date into your workbook.

1. **Key sentence:**
   The sentence should say *'Many of these girls come from England.'*
   Trace the sentence, filling in the blanks.
   Copy the sentence onto line 2.
   Now cover up the sentence and write it from dictation on line 3.

2. **Spelling patterns:**
   Read the words in Part 2. *(Prompt if necessary.)*
   Copy them onto line 2.
   Now cover your work and write them from dictation on line 3.

more	*store*	*wore*
tore	*sore*	*shore*

3. **Word sums:**
   Review morphemes *'less', 's'* and *'ing'.*
   Add these morphemes together:

welding	*rulers*	*thankless*
tables	*walking*	*moonless*

   Read the words you have written.
   Now turn the page and write the words from dictation.

4. **Filling in the blanks:**
   Trace the words, filling in the blanks.

super	*drift*	*should*
marble	*roam*	*pool*

5. **Morpheme analysis:**
   Fill in the blanks to show the morphemes in each word.

weld + ed	*cross + ed*	*smooth + ly*
mis + lead	*fear + less*	*wrong + ly*

6. Writing words:

super	*drift*	*should*
marble	*roam*	*pool*

7. Spelling test:

when	*brass*	*belt*	*tank*	*were*
soft	*there*	*summer*	*butter*	*drank*

8. Sentence dictation:

Every sentence must begin with a capital letter.

- What should every sentence begin with? **(A capital letter)**

(Repeat until firm)

Every sentence must end with a full stop or a question mark.

- What do you put at the end of a sentence?

(A full stop or a question mark)

1. *She wore a belt with her summer dress.*
2. *My father welded a brass bar to the gas tank.*
3. *There were five tubs of soft butter on the table.*
4. *When she was a little girl, my sister drank nothing but milk.*

Sentence 4 should have a comma. I will read the sentence again, you decide where the comma should go.

(Read the sentence ***without*** *exaggerating the pause.)*

9. Word bingo:

(See page 10 for instructions.)

table	*these*	*many*	*floating*
they	*thank*	*playful*	*girl*
dinner	*danger*	*walk*	*slight*
middle	*left*	*rifle*	*nothing*

(Write the day and the date on the white board—be sure to do this every day.)

Copy the day and the date into your workbook.

1. **Key sentence review:**
   Write the following sentences:

   1. *That is my duck.*
   2. *How much for fish and chips?*
   3. *I like to play with my little sister.*

2. **Spelling patterns:**
   You are going to write words spelled with *'qu'*, *'er'* and *'igh'*. When I say each word, point to the spelling pattern you will use and then write the word.

quit	*bright*	*better*	*serve*
tight	*sister*	*quilt*	*might*
quiz	*fight*	*queen*	*mother*

3. **Word sum dictation:**
   A morpheme is the smallest part of a word that has meaning.
   - What do we call the smallest part of a word that has meaning? **(A morpheme)**
   - What is the first morpheme in *miscall*? **(mis)**

   Write *mis* in the first blank in part 3.
   - What is the next morpheme in *miscall*? **(call)**

   Write *call* in the next blank.
   Now write *miscall* in the third blank.
   (Repeat for the following words:)

star + less = starless	*want + ed = wanted*
de + serve = deserve	*glass + es = glasses*
re + port = report	*strong + ly = strongly*
lead + er = leader	

3. Continued.
Now cover your work and write these words from dictation.

miscall	*starless*	*wanted*	*deserve*
glasses	*report*	*strongly*	*leader*

4. Copying the letters in words:
I'll spell some words and you write them down.
Then tell me what words I spelled.

quid	*letter*	*slight*
fright	*queen*	*serve*

Now cover your work and write these words again on the lines below. *(Dictate the words.)*

5. Word search:
Read the words before you start.

6. Spelling test:

try	*was*	*north*	*what*	*above*
how	*why*	*those*	*brown*	*stay*
shell	*much*	*wing*	*growl*	*pink*
torch	*they*	*save*	*stall*	*leave*
shy	*shark*	*speech*	*shook*	*along*

7. Word sums: *(Optional)*
Make at least eight real words from the following morphemes.
(Teacher may suggest words if necessary.)

de- mis- lay thank play -s -ed

(Write the day and the date on the white board—be sure to do this every day.)
Copy the day and the date into your workbook.

1. **New word introduction:**
(Write these words on a white board.)

train	*wait*	*word*
again	*trail*	*work*

Read each word and then spell it out loud.
(Prompt if necessary—then erase the words.)

Now spell the words out loud again.
(Dictate each word and write it on the board as the pupil(s) spell it, correcting errors—then erase the words.)

Now write the words in Part 1.
(Dictate the words in a different order.)

2. **Morpheme analysis:**
Read the words in Part 2.
Fill in the blanks to show the morphemes in each word.

un + load + ed	*bash + ful + ly*	*want + ed*
real + ly	*class + es*	*de + tail*
de + press + ing		

Now cover your work and write these words from dictation.

unloaded	*bashfully*	*wanted*
really	*classes*	*detail*
depressing		

3. **Sentence dictation using new words:**
Now you will write some sentences using the words you learned in Part 1.
All place names begin with a capital letter.
- What do place names begin with? **(A capital letter)**

The names of countries, cities and towns begin with a capital letter.
- What do the names of countries, cities and towns begin with? **(A capital letter)**

Green Bay is a city in America. *Green Bay* is two words.
- How many words are there in *Green Bay*? **(Two)**
- What will each one start with? **(A capital letter)**

1. *How long did you wait for the train to Green Bay?*

England is a country in Europe.
- What should *England* start with? **(A capital letter)**

2. *If you just say the word, I will fly to England.*

Sentence 2 should have a comma. I will read it again, you decide where the comma should go.

3. *Ken was working on the farm again.*

4. **Key sentence:**
The sentence should say *'I never use blue pencils.'*
Trace the sentence, filling in the blanks.
Copy the sentence onto line 2.
Now cover up the sentence and write it from dictation on line 3.

5. **Copying the letters in words:**
I'll spell some words and you write them down.
Then tell me what words I spelled.

silver *cattle* *nothing*

ladder *done* *danger*

Now cover your work and write these words again on the lines below. *(Dictate the words.)*

6. **Spelling patterns:**

   You are going to write words spelled with *'oa', 'ank'* and *'ore'*. When I say each word, point to the spelling pattern you will use and then write the word.

   coat drank more goat thank loaning

   Now write these sentences:

   1. Your goat drank all of my tea.

   2. There is nothing more to be done.

   3. Thank your sister for loaning me her coat.

1. **Key sentence:**
   The sentence should say *'I never use blue pencils.'*
   Trace the sentence, filling in the blanks.
   Copy the sentence onto line 2.
   Now cover up the sentence and write it from dictation on line 3.

2. **Spelling patterns:**
   Read the words in Part 2. *(Prompt if necessary.)*
   Copy them onto line 2.
   Now cover your work and write them from dictation on line 3.

world	*worst*	*rain*
worth	*worry*	*paid*

3. **Word sums:**
   New morpheme *'est'*.
   Add these morphemes together:

smallest	*strongest*	*cleanest*
brightest	*meanest*	*smoothest*

   Read the words you have written.
   Now turn the page and write the words from dictation.

4. **Filling in the blanks:**
   Trace the words, filling in the blanks.

done	*when*	*kind*	*England*
there	*trouble*	*who*	*Kent*

5. **Morpheme analysis:**
   Fill in the blanks to show the morphemes in each word.

kiss + es	*re + store*	*work + er*
re + tail	*float + ing*	*power + less*

6. Writing words:

done	*when*	*kind*	*England*
there	*trouble*	*who*	*Kent*

7. Spelling test:

train	*away*	*raft*	*pool*	*want*
silver	*many*	*wait*	*rubber*	*keep*

8. Sentence dictation:

All place names begin with a capital letter.

- What do place names begin with? **(A capital letter)**

The names of countries, cities and towns begin with a capital letter.

- What do the names of countries, cities and towns begin with? **(A capital letter)**

Little Rock is a city in America. *Little Rock* is two words.

- How many words are there in *Little Rock*? **(Two)**
- What will each word start with? **(A capital letter)**

1. *If it is raining, I do not want to wait for the train to Little Rock.*

Sentence 1 should have a comma. I will read the sentence again, you decide where the comma should go.

2. *Did your mother give you many kisses?*
3. *We keep our silver in the pool room.*
4. *Who is floating away on the rubber raft?*

9. Word bingo:

(See page 10 for instructions.)

fright	*queen*	*letter*	*serving*
pool	*should*	*marble*	*summer*
drift	*quilt*	*sister*	*leave*
speech	*those*	*speak*	*mother*

(Write the day and the date on the white board—be sure to do this every day.)

Copy the day and the date into your workbook.

1. **The vowel letters:**
   The vowel letters are *a, e, i, o* and *u.*
   Circle all the vowel letters on lines 1 and 2.

2. **The 'e' rule:**
   Find part 2 in your workbook. Listen carefully—this is a new rule.

   When a word ends with *'e'* and the next morpheme begins with a vowel, you must drop the *'e'*.

   - When do you drop the *'e'* from a word?
     (When the next morpheme begins with a vowel.)

   (Repeat until letter-perfect.)

3. **Word sums:**
   Look at Part 3 in your workbook.
   The first word-sum is *hope + ing*.
   - Does *ing* begin with a vowel? **(Yes)**
   - Do we drop the *'e'* when we write *hoping*? **(Yes)**
   - Spell *hoping* aloud. **(h-o-p-i-n-g)**

   The next word-sum is *hope + less*.
   - Does *less* begin with a vowel? **(No)**
   - Do we drop the *'e'* when we write *hopeless*? **(No)**

   Now write *hopeless.*

   Add the morphemes together.
   Remember the rule about dropping the *'e'*

   bravely *braver* *loving* *lovely*

4. Morpheme analysis—the *'e'* rule:

Look at Part 4 in your workbook. When you add *drive* and *ing,* you have to drop the *'e'* from *drive.*
So, when you take the word driving apart, you have to put the *'e'* back, there is no word spelled *d-r-i-v.*
Read the rest of the words in Part 4.
Fill in the blanks to show the morphemes in each word.

save + ing	*nice + est*	*please + ing*
come + ing	*serve + ed*	*use + er*

5. Word search:

Read the words before you start.

(Write the day and the date on the white board—be sure to do this every day.)

Copy the day and the date into your workbook.

1. **New word introduction:**

   (Write these words on a white board.)

   shout about nice our price loud

   Read each word and then spell it out loud.

   (Prompt if necessary—then erase the words.)

   Now spell the words out loud again.

   (Dictate each word and write it on the board as the pupil(s) spell it, correcting errors—then erase the words.)

   Now write the words in Part 1.

   (Dictate the words in a different order.)

2. **Word sums—the *'e'* rule:**

   Look at Part 2 in your workbook.

   The first word-sum is *serve + ing*.

   - Does *ing* begin with a vowel? **(Yes)**
   - Do we drop the *'e'* when we write *serving*? **(Yes)**

   Now write *serving*.

   The next word-sum is *like + ly*.

   - Does *ly* begin with a vowel? **(No)**
   - Do we drop the *'e'* when we write *likely*? **(No)**

   Now write *likely*.

   Now add the morphemes together.

   Some of them will follow the rule about dropping the *'e'*.

   hateful worrying maker

   worthless hopeless nicest

   Now cover your work and write these words from dictation.

3. Sentence dictation using new words:

You are going to write some sentences using the words you have just learned in Part 1.

The names of countries, cities and towns begin with a capital letter.

- What do the names of countries, cities and towns begin with? **(A capital letter)**

England is a country in Europe.

- What should *England* start with? **(A capital letter)**

1. *Did you read about our trip to England?*
2. *It is not nice to shout out loud.*
3. *What is the price of these rulers?*

4. Key sentence:

The sentence should say *'I never use blue pencils.'*
Trace the sentence, filling in the blanks.
Copy the sentence onto line 2.
Now cover up the sentence and write it from dictation on line 3.

5. Copying the letters in words:

I'll spell some words and you write them down.
Then tell me what words I spelled.

jungle	*butter*	*when*
marble	*super*	*driving*

Now cover your work and write these words again on the lines below. *(Dictate the words.)*

6. Spelling pattern review:

You are going to write words spelled with *'ai', 'alk'* and *'wor'*. When I say each word, point to the spelling pattern you will use and then write the word.

worth paid walked world rain worrying

Now write these sentences:

1. The girl walked bravely out in the rain.

2. It is not worth worrying about the danger.

3. That must be the worst paid work in the world.

Placement / Mastery Test:

Test to be used after Level 20:

(See the instructions for Mastery Tests on page 6.)

thankful	*summer*	*belt*	*store*	*choose*
killing	*worry*	*many*	*raining*	*these*
powerful	*banker*	*loader*	*reached*	*silver*
felt	*wore*	*kept*	*worst*	*fearless*

Scoring:

Mastery: *0-3 errors— pass*
4-7 errors— review spelling patterns and retest the the following day
8+ errors— go back to Level 11.

Placement: *0-2 errors— pass; start at this level, or go on to the next placement test*
2+ errors— start at Level 11, or go back to the placement test at the end of Level 10.

(At the beginning of each lesson, write the day and date on the white board. For instance, write ***Wednesday, 5 January 2011****.**)

At the beginning of each lesson, you will copy the day and date into your workbook. Write the day and the date in your workbook.

1. **Key sentence:**

   (On the first line the sentence is partially written in boxes, one box for each ***sound****—from Level 22 this changes to a blank for each missing letter. The pupil traces the sentence, filling in the empty boxes as he goes. Make sure he starts with a capital letter, has the right groups or individual letters in each box and finishes with a full stop. The pupil then copies the sentence onto line 2, check spelling and punctuation. Cover the work and dictate the sentence, if the pupil gets stuck or makes a mistake, show him the original.)*

   The sentence should say *'I never use blue pencils.'*

   Trace the sentence, filling in the blanks.

   Copy the sentence onto line 2.

   Now cover up the sentence and write it from dictation on line 3.

2. **Spelling patterns:**

   (New spelling patterns are introduced and tricky spellings reviewed in this exercise. Make sure the pupil has traced and copied correctly before covering and dictating. As with the Key Sentence; show him the original if he forgets the spelling.)

   Read the words in Part 2. *(Prompt if necessary.)*

   Copy them onto line 2.

   Now cover your work and write them from dictation on line 3.

ice	*nice*	*twice*
other	*brother*	*slice*

* Make this standard procedure for all written work. This is a simple and virtually fool-proof method of teaching children to spell the days and months. It is also essential training for writing formal letters.

3. Word sums—the *'e'* rule:

(This exercise introduces the morphemic principle in spelling. Pupils learn to spell the building blocks of more complex words and to join them together.)

Look at Part 3 in your workbook.

The first word-sum is *nice + ly*.

- Does *ly* begin with a vowel? **(No)**
- Do we drop the *'e'* when we write *nicely*? **(No)**

Now write *nicely*.

The next word-sum is *love + ed*.

- Does *ed* begin with a vowel? **(Yes)**
- Do we drop the *'e'* when we write *loved*? **(Yes)**

Now write *loved*.

Add the morphemes together.

Some of them will follow the rule about dropping the *'e'*.

stored	*loudest*	*used*
nicest	*bravely*	*worldly*

Now turn the page and write these words from dictation.

4. Filling in the blanks:

(The worksheet has a blank for each missing letter. Dictate each word and make sure the pupil traces the word and fills in each blank correctly as he goes.)

Trace the words, filling in the blanks.

nothing	*shore*	*gather*	*choose*
summer	*kid*	*kitchen*	*again*

5. Morpheme analysis:

(The reciprocal of ***Word Sums****. Pupils learn to identify the morphemes in words and to separate them.)*

Fill in the blanks to show the morphemes in each word.

give + ing	*come + ing*	*drive + er*
please + ed	*teach + er*	*price + less*

6. Writing words:

(This exercise recycles the words practised in ***Filling in the Blanks****. This time the pupil writes the words from dictation.)*

nothing	*shore*	*gather*	*choose*
summer	*kid*	*kitchen*	*again*

7. Spelling test:

(Dictate each word. If the pupil is confused by homophones such as be/bee, put the word in context.)

those	*girls*	*when*	*mice*	*these*
saw	*about*	*nice*	*who*	*coming*

8. Sentence dictation:

(Try to get the pupil to remember the whole sentence before he starts writing, as this will help to improve his memory. If he can't, dictate it in chunks—avoid dictating one word at a time.
The ***Spelling Test*** *and* ***Sentence Dictation*** *should always be done at one sitting, if at all possible, as the spelling test rehearses words used in the dictation, which may be forgotten by the next day.)*

1. *They say that nice dress is priceless.*
2. *Our teacher was talking about mice again.*
3. *Who saw those girls over there?*

The next sentence should have a comma. This time, I will not repeat the sentence after you have written it, so listen carefully.

4. *After the game, these boys are coming back for dinner.*

9. Word search:

(Pupils should read the words in the puzzle before they start. Imposing a time limit prevents the pupil using it to waste time.)

Read the words before you start.

(Write the day and the date on the white board—be sure to do this every day.)
Copy the day and the date into your workbook.

1. **New word introduction:**
   (Write these words on a white board.)

   cage count page age house south

   Read each word and then spell it out loud.
   (Prompt if necessary—then erase the words.)

   Now spell the words out loud again.
   (Dictate each word and write it on the board as the pupil(s) spell it, correcting errors—then erase the words.)

   Now write the words in Part 1.
   (Dictate the words in a different order.)

2. **Word sums—the *'e'* rule:**
   Look at Part 2 in your workbook.
   The first word-sum is *have + ing*.
   - Does *ing* begin with a vowel? **(Yes)**
   - Do we drop the *'e'* when we write *having*? **(Yes)**

   Now write *having*.

   The next word-sum is *snore + ing*.
   - Does *ing* begin with a vowel? **(Yes)**
   - Do we drop the *'e'* when we write *snoring*? **(Yes)**

   Now write *snoring*.

   Add the morphemes together.
   Some of them will follow the rule about dropping the *'e'*.

   cleanest pager worthless

   hopeless brotherly aging

   Now cover your work and write these words from dictation.

3. **Key sentence:**
   The sentence should say *'Some people are always happy.'*
   Trace the sentence, filling in the blanks.
   Copy the sentence onto line 2.
   Now cover up the sentence and write it from dictation on line 3.

4. Sentence dictation using new words:

Now you will write some sentences using the words you learned in Part 1.

The names of countries, counties and cities begin with a capital letter.

- What do the names of countries, counties and cities begin with?

(A capital letter)

Kent is a county in England.

- What should Kent start with? **(A capital letter)**

1. *When do you want to fly south to Kent?*
2. *At our house we keep mice in a cage.*
3. *Can you count all the pages in that book?*

5. Copying the letters in words:

I'll spell some words and you write them down.

Then tell me what words I spelled.

girls	*know*	*when*
these	*said*	*talk*

Now cover your work and write these words again on the lines below. *(Dictate the words.)*

6. Spelling patterns:

You are going to write words spelled with *'oa'*, *'ai'* and *'ou'*. When I say each word, point to the spelling pattern you will use and then write the word.

south *again* *toad* *train* *goat* *our*

Now write these sentences:

1. *The paper got left out in the rain again.*
2. *Our goat is bigger than your little toad.*
3. *Last summer we took a train going south.*

(Write the day and the date on the white board—be sure to do this every day.)
Copy the day and the date into your workbook.

1. **Key sentence:**
   The sentence should say *'Some people are always happy.'*
   Trace the sentence, filling in the blanks.
   Copy the sentence onto line 2.
   Now cover up the sentence and write it from dictation on line 3.

2. **Spelling patterns:**
   Read the words in Part 2. *(Prompt if necessary.)*
   Copy them onto line 2.
   Now cover your work and write them from dictation on line 3.

loaf	*find*	*mind*
goal	*kind*	*behind*

3. **Word sums—the *'e'* rule:**
   Look at Part 3 in your workbook.
   The first word-sum is *age + less*.
   - Does *less* begin with a vowel? **(No)**
   - Do we drop the *'e'* when we write *ageless*? **(No)**

   Now write *ageless*.

   The next word-sum is *page + ing*.
   - Does *ing* begin with a vowel? **(Yes)**
   - Do we drop the *'e'* when we write *paging*? **(Yes)**

   Now write *paging*.

   Add the morphemes together.
   Some of them will follow the rule about dropping the *'e'*.

kindest	*fearless*	*slicer*
thinker	*nicest*	*mindless*

   Now cover your work and write these words from dictation.

4. **Filling in the blanks:**
   Trace the words, filling in the blanks.

brother	*danger*	*talking*
many	*skill*	*worst*

5. Morpheme analysis:
Fill in the blanks to show the morphemes in each word.

keep + ing	*power + ful*	*make + ing*
nice + ly	*please + ed*	*de + serve + ing*

6. Writing words:

brother	*danger*	*talking*
many	*skill*	*worst*

7. Spelling test:

house	*toad*	*work*	*girl*	*would*
goat	*other*	*our*	*please*	*about*

8. Sentence dictation:
Every sentence must begin with a capital letter.
- What should every sentence begin with? **(A capital letter)**

Every sentence must end with a full stop or a question mark.
- What do you put at the end of a sentence?
  (A full stop or a question mark)

1. *They were far behind with the work.*
2. *Would you mind keeping a toad for our girl?*
3. *Your goat is making a mess of her house.*

The next sentence should have a comma, so listen carefully.

4. *Could you find out about the other pencils, please?*

9. Word search:
Read the words before you start.

(Write the day and the date on the white board—be sure to do this every day.)

Copy the day and the date into your workbook.

1. **New word introduction:**
   (Write these words on a white board.)

   gang soak rang sang moan hang

   Read each word and then spell it out loud.
   (Prompt if necessary—then erase the words.)

   Now spell the words out loud again.
   (Dictate each word and write it on the board as the pupil(s) spell it, correcting errors—then erase the words.)

   Now write the words in Part 1.
   (Dictate the words in a different order.)

2. **Morpheme analysis:**
   Read the words in Part 2.
   Fill in the blanks to show the morphemes in each word.

soak + ing	*price + ed*	*un + kind*
walk + ing	*trouble + ed*	*count + er*

   Now cover your work and write these words on the lines below.

soaking	*priced*	*unkind*
walking	*troubled*	*counter*

3. **Key sentence:**
   The sentence should say *'Some people are always happy.'*
   Trace the sentence, filling in the blanks.
   Copy the sentence onto line 2.
   Now cover up the sentence and write it from dictation on line 3.

4. **Sentence dictation using new words:**
   You are going to write some sentences using the words you have just learned in Part 1. Listen for the commas.

   1. *Our gang likes to hang out behind the store.*
   2. *When I rang her up, she had a good moan.*
   3. *They got a good soaking, walking in the rain*

5. Copying the letters in words:

I'll spell some words and you write them down.
Then tell me what words I spelled.

silver	*cattle*	*nothing*
ladder	*done*	*danger*

Now cover your work and write these words again on the lines below. *(Dictate the words.)*

6. Spelling pattern review:

You are going to write words spelled with *'ice'*, *'age'* and *'ore'*. When I say each word, point to the spelling pattern you will use and then write the word.

more	*nice*	*pages*
price	*wore*	*slicer*

Now write these sentences:

1. *You could read more pages in a better light.*
2. *My sister wore a nice pink dress to the ball.*
3. *What is the price of that meat slicer?*

7. Spelling patterns:

Read the words in Part 7. *Prompt if necessary.)*
Copy them onto line 2.
Now cover your work and write them from dictation on line 3.

skid	*skip*	*skill*	*skin*
skit	*skim*	*sky*	*skimp*

(Write the day and date on the white board—be sure to do this every day.)
Copy the day and date into your workbook.

1. **Key sentence review:**
   Write the following sentences:

   1. *We eat oats out of a bowl.*
   2. *Would you make some tea, please?*
   3. *Put your hat on when you are done.*

2. **Spelling patterns:**
   You are going to write words spelled with *'x'*, *'ss'* and *'ea'*.
   When I say each word, point to the spelling pattern you will use and then write the word.

foxes	*press*	*read*	*fixed*
cross	*mixer*	*kisses*	*yearly*
speak	*six*	*pass*	*leaving*

3. **Word sum dictation:**
   A morpheme is the smallest part of a word that has meaning.
   - What do we call the smallest part of a word that has meaning? **(A morpheme)**
   - What is the first morpheme in *worthless*? **(worth)**

   Write *worth* in the first blank in part 3.
   - What is the next morpheme in *worthless*? **(less)**

   Write *less* in the next blank.
   Now write *worthless* in the third blank.
   (Repeat for the following words.)

lunch + es = lunches	*mean + est = meanest*
de + serve = deserve	*want + ed = wanted*
mis + call = miscall	*re + took = retook*
moon + less = moonless	

3. Continued:
Now cover your work and write these words from dictation.

worthless *lunches* *meanest* *deserve*

wanted *miscall* *retook* *moonless*

4. Copying the letters in words:
I'll spell some words and you write them down.
Then tell me what words I spelled.

word *above* *crown*

better *bright* *drying*

Now cover your work and write these words again on the lines below. *(Dictate the words.)*

5. Crossword:
Read the words before you start.

6. Spelling test:

said	*make*	*walk*	*there*	*trouble*
done	*when*	*town*	*know*	*what*
brass	*stall*	*boot*	*girl*	*wrong*
growl	*were*	*some*	*many*	*shook*
these	*came*	*blue*	*who*	*England*

7. Word sums: *(Optional)*
Make at least eight real words from the following morphemes.
(Teacher may suggest words if necessary.)

un- *love* *load* *save* *-ing* *-er* *-ed*

Sentence dictation:

See page 30 for instructions.

All place names begin with a capital letter.

- What do all names begin with? **(A capital letter)**

Bonus points for spotting the commas!

1. *We got paid for working in Spain last summer.*
2. *Do you think that England will ever win the World Cup?*
3. *When is my brother coming to dinner again?*
4. *I always worry about making the train to Fleet Street.*
5. *Many of those girls have never used soap.*
6. *Some people are waiting for the Queen behind our house.*
7. *The King was counting all of his pencils and rubbers.*
8. *My blue coat got soaked in the rain.*
9. *Would you cut another slice off the loaf, please?*
10. *I never worry about my work.*
11. *How many words are on this page?*
12. *Could I have some more butter, please?*

(Write the day and the date on the white board—be sure to do this every day.)

Copy the day and the date into your workbook.

1. **New word introduction:**
   (Write these words on a white board.)

   bird stir damp tramp shirt

   Read each word and then spell it out loud.
   (Prompt if necessary—then erase the words.)

   Now spell the words out loud again.
   (Dictate each word and write it on the board as the pupil(s) spell it, correcting errors—then erase the words.)

   Now write the words in Part 1.
   (Dictate the words in a different order.)

2. **Morpheme analysis:**
   Read the words in Part 2.

save + ing	*give + er*	*store + ing*
cross + es	*power + less*	*hate + ful*
right + ful + ly	*use + less*	

   Now cover your work and write these words on lines below.

saving	*giver*	*storing*	*crosses*
powerless	*hateful*	*rightfully*	*useless*

3. **Key sentence:**
   The sentence should say *'Does she have very many rabbits?'*
   Trace the sentence, filling in the blanks.
   Copy the sentence onto line 2.
   Now cover up the sentence and write it from dictation on line 3.

4. **Sentence dictation using new words:**
You are going to write some sentences using the words you have just learned in Part 1.

1. *Why is my blue shirt still damp?*
2. *That is the first bird I have seen this year.*
3. *I saw the tramp stir his tea.*

5. **Copying the letters in words:**
I'll spell some words and you write them down. Then tell me what words I spelled.

bigger	*always*	*there*
people	*skip*	*gather*

Now cover your work and write these words again on the lines below. *(Dictate the words.)*

6. **Spelling pattern review:**
You are going to write words spelled with *'ai',* *'wor'* and *'ou'.* When I say each word, point to the spelling pattern you will use and then write the word.

rain	*about*	*worth*
train	*house*	*worry*

Now write these sentences:

1. *How much is your house worth?*
2. *Do not worry about the rain.*
3. *Some people always go by train.*

Apples and Pears Level 28:

(Write the day and the date on the white board—be sure to do this every day.)

Copy the day and the date into your workbook.

1. **Key sentence:**
   The sentence should say *'Does she have very many rabbits?'*
   Trace the sentence, filling in the blanks.
   Copy the sentence onto line 2.
   Now cover up the sentence and write it from dictation on line 3.

2. **Spelling patterns:**
   Read the words in Part 2. *(Prompt if necessary.)*
   Copy them onto line 2.
   Now cover your work and write them from dictation on line 3.

most	*ghost*	*rice*
post	*spice*	*almost*

3. **Word sums:**
   New morpheme *'en'*.
   Add these morphemes together:

lighten	*wooden*	*sweeten*
fallen	*dampen*	*frighten*

   Read the words you have written.
   Now cover your work and write the words from dictation.

4. **Filling in the blanks:**
   Trace the words, filling in the blanks.

after	*people*	*brown*
broom	*trouble*	*wrong*

5. **Morpheme analysis:**
   Fill in the blanks to show the morphemes in each word.

clean + er	*cook + ed*	*reach + ed*
to + night	*fall + en*	*beat + en*

6. Writing words:

after	*people*	*brown*
broom	*trouble*	*wrong*

7. Spelling test:

tramp	*wore*	*letters*	*there*	*said*
saw	*these*	*storm*	*some*	*after*

8. Sentence dictation:

All names and titles begin with a capital letter.

- What do all names and titles begin with? **(A capital letter)**

1. *I will post some of these letters to Miss Brown tonight.*
2. *Rice cooked with spice is very nice.*
3. *The tramp said that he saw a ghost.*

The next sentence should have a comma, so listen carefully.

4. *After the storm was over, there were a lot of fallen trees.*

9. Word bingo:

(See page 10 for instructions.)

shout	*world*	*unpaid*	*our*
blue	*jungle*	*super*	*when*
danger	*who*	*nice*	*worry*
read	*worth*	*ruler*	*talk*

(Write the day and the date on the white board—be sure to do this every day.)

Copy the day and the date into your workbook.

1. **New word introduction:**
   (Write these words on a white board.)

   stamp sail camp plain afraid lamp

   Read each word and then spell it out loud.
   (Prompt if necessary—then erase the words.)

   Now spell the words out loud again.
   (Dictate each word and write it on the board as the pupil(s) spell it, correcting errors—then erase the words.)

   Now write the words in Part 1.
   (Dictate the words in a different order.)

2. **Morpheme analysis:**
   Read the words in Part 3.
   Fill in the blanks to show the morphemes in each word.

week + end	*leave + ing*	*act + ing*
howl + ed	*score + ing*	*make + ing*

   Now cover your work and write these words from dictation.

weekend	*leaving*	*acting*
howled	*scoring*	*making*

3. **Sentence dictation using new words:**
   Now you will write some sentences using the words you learned in Part 1. Listen for the comma.

   1. *It is all plain sailing from now on.*
   2. *If you give me a stamp, I will post your letter.*
   3. *I am afraid we will not go camping this weekend.*

4. **Key sentence:**
   The sentence should say *'Does she have very many rabbits?'*
   Trace the sentence, filling in the blanks.
   Copy the sentence onto line 2.
   Now cover up the sentence and write it from dictation on line 3.

5. **Copying the letters in words:**
   I'll spell some words and you write them down.
   Then tell me what words I spelled.

skill	*worst*	*people*
other	*shrink*	*scrap*

   Now cover your work and write these words again on the lines below. *(Dictate the words.)*

6. **Spelling patterns:**
   You are going to write words spelled with *'oa', 'ind'* and *'age'*. When I say each word, point to the spelling pattern you will use and then write the word.

find	*stage*	*coat*
age	*toads*	*mind*

   Now write these sentences:

   1. At your age I was acting on the stage.

   2. Did the girl find very many toads?

   3. Would you mind loaning me your blue coat?

Apples and Pears Level 30:

(Write the day and the date on the white board—be sure to do this every day.)

Copy the day and the date into your workbook.

1. **Key sentence review:**
   Write the following sentences:

   1. *I like to play with my little sister.*
   2. *Do you know what my father said?*
   3. *We saw who came over.*

2. **Spelling patterns:**
   You are going to write words spelled with *'and', 'ss'* and *'oo'*. When I say each word, point to the spelling pattern you will use and then write the word.

stand	*bliss*	*brand*	*moon*
school	*choose*	*loss*	*land*
press	*grand*	*stress*	*smooth*

3. **Word sum dictation:**
   A morpheme is the smallest part of a word that has meaning.
   - What do we call the smallest part of a word that has meaning? **(A morpheme)**
   - What is the first morpheme in *powerful*? **(power)**

   Write *power* in the first blank in part 3.
   - What is the next morpheme in *powerful*? **(ful)**

   Write *ful* in the next blank.
   Now write *powerful* in the third blank.
   (Repeat for the following words:)

loud + ly = loudly	*un + happy = unhappy*
re + tail = retail	*roam + ing = roaming*
wood + en = wooden	*class + es = classes*
brother + ly = brotherly	

3. Continued:

Now turn the page and write these words from dictation.

powerful	*loudly*	*unhappy*	*retail*
roaming	*wooden*	*classes*	*brotherly*

4. Copying the letters in words:

I'll spell some words and you write them down.
Then tell me what words I spelled.

team	*quiz*	*above*
away	*rather*	*cattle*

Now cover your work and write these words again on the lines below. *(Dictate the words.)*

5. Word search:

Read the words before you start.

6. Spelling test:

these	*why*	*super*	*use*	*from*
people	*what*	*rifle*	*some*	*girls*
when	*marble*	*butter*	*was*	*never*
many	*those*	*pencil*	*bigger*	*want*
ruler	*done*	*blue*	*always*	*who*

7. Word sums: *(Optional)*

Make at least eight real words from the following morphemes.
(Teacher may suggest words if necessary.)

un- *brave* *load* *kind* *-ing* *-ly* *-est*

Test to be used after Level 30:

(See the instructions for Mastery Tests on page 6.)

loudly	*nicest*	*priced*	*counting*	*about*
does	*south*	*kindly*	*moan*	*always*
pager	*mostly*	*people*	*first*	*damp*
very	*hopeless*	*giving*	*loafer*	*hanger*

Scoring:

Mastery: *0-3 errors— pass*
4-7 errors— review spelling patterns and retest the following day
8+ errors— go back to Level 21.

Placement: *0-2 errors— pass; start at this level, or go on to the next placement test*
2+ errors— start at Level 21, or go back to the placement test at the end of Level 20.

(At the beginning of each lesson, write the day and date on the white board. For instance, write ***Wednesday, 5 January 2011****.** *)*

At the beginning of each lesson, you will copy the day and date into your workbook. Write the day and the date in your workbook.

1. **Contractions—*can't*:**

   You are going to learn how to spell contractions.
   Look at Part 1 in your workbook.
   The words *can* and *not* can be shortened to *can't*.
   The word *can't* is a contraction.
   The little squiggle between the *n* and the *t* is called an apostrophe.
   • What is it called? **(An apostrophe)**
   (If the pupil has problems pronouncing 'apostrophe', break it down into a/pos/troh/fee.)

   Now I am going to spell *can't—c-a-n* apostrophe *t*.
   • Spell *can't* aloud. **(c-a-n apostrophe t)**
   Copy *can't* onto the line next to the word.
   Cover up your work and write *can't* on the line below.

2. **Contractions—*don't*:**

   Look at Part 2 in your workbook.
   The words *do* and *not* can be shortened to *don't*.
   • Spell *don't* aloud. **(d-o-n apostrophe t)**
   Copy *don't* onto the line next to the word.
   Cover your work and write *don't* on the line below.

3. **Contractions—*it's*:**

   Look at Part 3 in your workbook.
   The words *it* and *is* can be shortened to *it's*.
   • Spell *it's* aloud. **(i-t apostrophe s)**
   Copy *it's* onto the line next to the word.
   Cover your work and write *it's* on the line below.

---

* Make this standard procedure for all written work. This is a simple and virtually fool-proof method of teaching children to spell the days and months. It is also essential training for writing formal letters.

4. Contractions—*I've*:

Look at Part 4 in your workbook.

The words *I* and *have* can be shortened to *I've*.

- Spell *I've* aloud. **(I apostrophe v-e)**

Copy *I've* onto the line next to the word.

Cover your work and write *I've* on the line below.

5. Dictation sentences:

Write these sentences in Part 5.

1. *I can't go out tonight.*
2. *Don't be a fool!*
3. *It's a nice day.*
4. *I've got a lot of work to do.*

(Write the day and the date on the white board—be sure to do this every day.)

Copy the day and the date into your workbook.

1. **New word introduction:**

   (Write these words on a white board.)

   mouse toy enjoy destroy cloud mouth

   Read each word and then spell it out loud.

   (Prompt if necessary—then erase the words.)

   Now spell the words out loud again.

   (Dictate each word and write it on the board as the pupil(s) spell it, correcting errors—then erase the words.)

   Now write the words in Part 1.

   (Dictate the words in a different order.)

2. **Morpheme analysis:**

   (In this exercise pupils learn to identify the morphemes in words and to separate them.)

   Read the words in Part 2.

   Fill in the blanks to show the morphemes in each word.

wood + en	*lamp + post*	*leave + ing*
score + ed	*fright + en*	*glass + es*

   Now cover your work and write these words from dictation.

wooden	*lamppost*	*leaving*
scored	*frighten*	*glasses*

3. **Sentence dictation using new words:**

   (Try to get the pupil to remember the whole sentence before he starts writing, as this will help to improve his memory. If he can't, dictate it in chunks—avoid dictating one word at a time.)

   Now you will write some sentences using the words you learned in Part 1.

   1. *The bad boy destroyed my toys.*
   2. *My cat enjoys playing with his mouse.*
   3. *How many teeth are in your mouth?*

4. **Key sentence:**

(On the first line the sentence is partially written with a blank for each missing letter The pupil traces the sentence, filling in the blanks as he goes. Make sure he starts with a capital letter, spells each word correctly and finishes with a question mark. The pupil then copies the sentence onto line 2, check spelling and punctuation. Cover the work and dictate the sentence, if the pupil gets stuck or makes a mistake, show him the original.)

The sentence should say *'Which one should we buy?'.*

Trace the sentence, filling in the blanks.

Copy the sentence onto line 2.

Now cover up the sentence and write it from dictation on line 3.

5. **Copying the letters in words:**

I'll spell some words and you write them down.

Then tell me what words I spelled.

I've	*very*	*can't*
skip	*don't*	*does*

Now cover your work and write these words again on the lines below. *(Dictate the words.)*

6. **Spelling patterns:**

You are going to write words spelled with *'ost'*, *'ir'* and *'amp'*.

When I say each word, point to the spelling pattern you will use and then write the word.

almost	*girl*	*camping*
skirt	*first*	*lamppost*

Now write these sentences:

1. *Don't run your car into the lamppost.*
2. *Does your girl want to go camping?*
3. *We almost got there first.*

(Write the day and the date on the white board—be sure to do this every day.)

Copy the day and the date into your workbook.

1. **Key sentence:**
   The sentence should say *'Which one should we buy?'*
   Trace the sentence, filling in the blanks.
   Copy the sentence onto line 2.
   Now cover up the sentence and write it from dictation on line 3.

2. **Spelling patterns:**
   (New spelling patterns are introduced and tricky spellings reviewed in this exercise. Make sure the pupil has copied correctly before covering and dictating. As with the Key Sentence; show him the original if he forgets the spelling.)
   Read the words in Part 2. *(Prompt if necessary.)*
   Copy them onto line 2.
   Now cover your work and write them from dictation on line 3.

   junk *sunk* *face*

   race *place* *space*

3. **Word sums:**
   (This exercise introduces the morphemic principle in spelling. Pupils learn to spell the building blocks of more complex words and to join them together.)
   Review morphemes *'en', 'ed'* and *'mis'*
   Add these morphemes together:

   misplaced *priced* *frighten*

   pleased *mislay* *wooden*

   Read the words you have written.
   Now cover your work and write the words from dictation.

4. **Filling in the blanks:**
(The worksheet has a blank for each missing letter. Dictate each word and make sure the pupil traces the word and fills in each blank correctly as he goes.)
Trace the words, filling in the blanks.

does	*drift*	*middle*
hang	*kilt*	*trouble*

5. **Morpheme analysis:**
Fill in the blanks to show the morphemes in each word.

cook + ing	*most + ly*	*to + day*
mix + es	*fear + less*	*dog + house*

6. **Writing words:**
(This exercise recycles the words practised in ***Filling in the Blanks****. This time the pupil writes the words from dictation.)*

does	*drift*	*middle*
hang	*kilt*	*trouble*

7. **Spelling test:**
(Dictate each word. If the pupil is confused by homophones such as be/bee, put the word in context.)

clean	*enjoy*	*don't*	*can't*	*does*
make	*very*	*house*	*shirt*	*meals*

8. Sentence dictation:

(Try to get the pupil to remember the whole sentence before he starts writing, as this will help to improve his memory. If he can't, dictate it in chunks—avoid dictating one word at a time.

The ***Spelling Test*** *and* ***Sentence Dictation*** *should always be done at one sitting, if at all possible, as the spelling test rehearses words used in the dictation, which may be forgotten by the next day.)*

All names and titles begin with a capital letter.

- What do all names and titles begin with? **(A capital letter)**

1. *Does the tramp enjoy cooking meals for the Queen?*
2. *Please don't let Mark frighten my little rabbits.*
3. *My father knows how to make wooden boats.*

This sentence should have a comma, so listen carefully.

4. *If you can't find any clean shirts, come to our house.*

9. Word bingo:

(See page 10 for instructions.)

slice	*pages*	*worry*	*mice*
more	*light*	*score*	*skill*
oats	*please*	*put*	*bowler*
word	*better*	*mixes*	*wrong*

(Write the day and the date on the white board—be sure to do this every day.)

Copy the day and the date into your workbook.

1. **New word introduction:**

   (Write these words on a white board.)

   found round around old cold sound

   Read each word and then spell it out loud.
   (Prompt if necessary—then erase the words.)

   Now spell the words out loud again.
   (Dictate each word and write it on the board as the pupil(s) spell it, correcting errors—then erase the words.)

   Now write the words in Part 1.
   (Dictate the words in a different order.)

2. **Morpheme analysis:**

   Read the words in Part 2.
   Fill in the blanks to show the morphemes in each word.

box + es	*walk + ing*	*dinner + s*
lift + ed	*come + ing*	*race + er*

   Now cover your work and write these words from dictation.

boxes	*walking*	*dinners*
lifted	*coming*	*racer*

3. **Sentence dictation using new words:**

   Every sentence must begin with a capital letter.
   - What should every sentence begin with? **(A capital letter)**

   Every sentence must end with a full stop or a question mark.
   - What do you put at the end of a sentence?
     (A full stop or a question mark)

   Now you will write some sentences using the words you learned in Part 1.

   1. *It's very cold round at our house.*
   2. *The little girl can't stand loud sounds.*
   3. *The old tramp has not found the round boxes.*

4. Key sentence:
The sentence should say *'Which one should we buy?'*
Trace the sentence, filling in the blanks.
Copy the sentence onto line 2.
Now cover up the sentence and write it from dictation on line 3.

5. Copying the letters in words:
I'll spell some words and you write them down.
Then tell me what words I spelled.

goals	*team*	*went*
many	*moon*	*don't*

Now cover your work and write these words again on the lines below. *(Dictate the words.)*

6. Spelling patterns:
You are going to write words spelled with *'ice'*, *'or'* and *'ace'*. When I say each word, point to the spelling pattern you will use and then write the word.

twice	*place*	*more*
space	*mice*	*scored*

Now write these sentences:

1. *The spaceship went around the moon twice.*
2. *Our team scored more goals than yours.*
3. *We don't have many mice around our place.*

Level 35:

(Write the day and the date on the white board—be sure to do this every day.)

Copy the day and the date into your workbook.

1. **Key sentence review:**
   Write the following sentences:

   1. *Put your hat on when you are done.*
   2. *There is nothing on the table for dinner.*
   3. *I never use blue pencils.*

2. **Spelling patterns:**
   You are going to write words spelled with *'oa', 'er'* and *'ft'*. When I say each word, point to the spelling pattern you will use and then write the word.

road	*lift*	*coat*	*ladder*
raft	*danger*	*load*	*left*
soap	*rather*	*soft*	*gather*

3. **Word sum dictation:**
   A morpheme is the smallest part of a word that has meaning.
   - What do we call the smallest part of a word that has meaning? **(A morpheme)**
   - What is the first morpheme in *strongest?* **(strong)**

   Write *strong* in the first blank in Part 3.
   - What is the next morpheme in *strongest?* **(est)**

   Write *est* in the next blank.
   Now write *strongest* in the third blank.
   (Repeat for the following words:)

want + ing = wanting	*un + real = unreal*
speak + er = speaker	*cord + less = cordless*
fast + en = fasten	*de + part + ing = departing*
bright + en + ed = brightened	

3. Continued:

Now turn the page and write these words from dictation.

strongest	*wanting*	*unreal*	*speaker*
cordless	*fasten*	*departing*	*brightened*

4. Copying the letters in words:

I'll spell some words and you write them down.
Then tell me what words I spelled.

thank	*talk*	*belt*
shore	*least*	*spend*

Now cover your work and write these words again on the lines below. *(Dictate the words.)*

5. Crossword:

(Pupils should read the words in the puzzle before they start. Imposing a time limit prevents the pupil using it to waste time.)

Read the words before you start.

6. Spelling test:

skin	*quack*	*what*	*from*	*wrong*
which	*scar*	*after*	*why*	*school*
afraid	*who*	*scab*	*when*	*almost*
work	*about*	*want*	*skip*	*always*
were	*was*	*keg*	*above*	*around*

7. Word sums: *(Optional)*

Make at least 8 real words from the following morphemes.
(Teacher may suggest words if necessary.)

de- *tail* *press* *form* *-er* *-less* *-es*

Sentence dictation:

See page 30 for instructions.

All place names begin with a capital letter.

- What do all names begin with? **(A capital letter)**

Bonus points for spotting the commas!

1. *Which bird did you see flying south to Spain?*
2. *Don't worry about those people from West Ham.*
3. *The old sailboat almost sank last night.*
4. *I gather the old tramp got left behind in Hull.*
5. *Please hang your shirt out to dry, if it is still damp.*
6. *I don't know if the ghost still hangs around our house.*
7. *I've loaded most of the junk onto the train to Leeds.*
8. *You can't buy very many stamps for a pound.*
9. *We need more space in our bedroom.*
10. *If you are standing out in the rain, you will get soaked.*
11. *My brown rabbit took first place in the sack race.*
12. *Does your mouse enjoy eating butter?*

Did you use a comma in any of these sentences?
(Give a special star to every pupil who gets it right.)

1. **Silent *'e'*:**

You are going to write some words that end with the letter *'e'*.

- What letter will these words end with? **('e')**

Listen to each word and you will hear a letter name.

The first word is *hate*.

- What letter name do you hear in *hate*? **(A)**

Now write *hate*.

The next word is *time*.

- What letter name do you hear in *time*? **(I)**

Write *time*.

(Repeat this procedure for the following words:)

hope	*tune*	*game*	*coke*	*ride*
cure	*home*	*lake*	*size*	*mine*

2. **Word sum dictation:**

- What is the first morpheme in *homeless*? **(home)**

Write *home* in the first blank in Part 2.

- What is the next morpheme in *homeless*? **(less)**

Write *less* in the next blank.

Now write *homeless* in the third blank.

Remember the rule about dropping the *'e'*.

(Repeat for the following words:)

hope + ing = hoping

tune + er = tuner

time + ed = timed

game + ly = gamely

tune + ed = tuned

ride + ing = riding

hope + ful = hopeful

cure + ed = cured

hate + ed = hated

Now cover your work and write these words from dictation.

homeless	*hoping*	*riding*	*tuner*	*hopeful*
timed	*cured*	*gamely*	*hated*	*tuned*

3. Writing words:

Write these silent *'e'* words:

like	*make*	*came*	*drive*	*wave*
nice	*cage*	*place*	*rice*	*face*

4. Sentence dictation:

All names and titles begin with a capital letter.

- What do all names and titles begin with? **(A capital letter)**

All brand names begin with a capital letter.

- What do all brand names begin with? **(A capital letter)**

Coke is a brand name.

- What should *Coke* begin with? **(A capital letter)**

Write the following sentences:

1. *Mother said we could drink some Coke now.*
2. *Miss Clay always likes riding the brown horse.*
3. *Has Lord North found a cure for his cold?*
4. *I was hoping to be there by noon.*

5. Word bingo:

(See page 10 for instructions.)

jungle	*butter*	*when*	*twice*
brother	*count*	*page*	*mice*
house	*always*	*these*	*talk*
toad	*behind*	*loaf*	*kind*

Apples and Pears Level 38:

(Write the day and the date on the white board—be sure to do this every day.)

Copy the day and the date into your workbook.

1. **New word introduction:**

   (Write these words on a white board.)

   hold warm warn told sold fold

   Read each word and then spell it out loud.

   (Prompt if necessary—then erase the words.)

   Now spell the words out loud again.

   (Dictate each word and write it on the board as the pupil(s) spell it, correcting errors—then erase the words.)

   Now write the words in Part 1.

   (Dictate the words in a different order.)

2. **Morpheme analysis:**

   Read the words in Part 2.

   Fill in the blanks to show the morphemes in each word.

cure + ed	*hope + ing*	*swan + s*
wood + en	*un + load*	*light + est*

Now cover your work and write these words from dictation.

cured	*hoping*	*swans*
wooden	*unload*	*lightest*

3. **Sentence dictation using new words:**

   Now you will write some sentences using the words you learned in Part 1. Listen for the comma.

   1. *I told you that we sold our house.*
   2. *My mother warned you about those girls.*
   3. *If I hold your hand, it will stay warm.*

4. **Key sentence:**
   The sentence should say *'The Queen has two hundred swans in her front garden.'*
   Trace the sentence, filling in the blanks.
   Copy the sentence onto line 2.
   Now cover up the sentence and write it from dictation on line 3.

5. **Copying the letters in words:**
   I'll spell some words and you write them down.
   Then tell me what words I spelled.

worst	*lake*	*plain*
does	*mine*	*trouble*

   Now cover your work and write these words again on the lines below. *(Dictate the words.)*

6. **Spelling patterns:**
   You are going to write words spelled with *'-le', 'wor'* and *'ai'.* When I say each word, point to the spelling pattern you will use and then write the word.

marble	*worth*	*again*
trouble	*sail*	*world*

   Now write these sentences.

   1. How much is that nice marble worth?

   2. We had some trouble working on the little table.

   3. I'm afraid I can't wait to sail around the world again.

Apples and Pears Level 39:

(Write the day and the date on the white board—be sure to do this every day.)
Copy the day and the date into your workbook.

1. **Key sentence:**
   The sentence should say *'The Queen has two hundred swans in her front garden.'*
   Trace the sentence, filling in the blanks.
   Copy the sentence onto line 2.
   Now cover up the sentence and write it from dictation on line 3.

2. **Spelling patterns:**
   Read the words in Part 2. *(Prompt if necessary.)*
   Copy them onto line 2.
   Now cover your work and write them from dictation on line 3.

dump	*jump*	*lump*
ground	*pound*	*trunk*

3. **Word sums:**
   New morphemes *'able'*
   Add these morphemes together:

sizable	*curable*	*drivable*
foldable	*workable*	*enjoyable*

   Read the words you have written.
   Now turn the page and write the words from dictation.

4. **Filling in the blanks:**
   Trace the words, filling in the blanks.

there	*never*	*happy*
summer	*destroy*	*danger*

5. **Morpheme analysis:**
Fill in the blanks to show the morphemes in each word.

soft + en	*clean + est*	*de + serve*
toss + ed	*box + es*	*power + ful*

6. **Writing words:**

there	*never*	*happy*
summer	*destroy*	*danger*

7. **Spelling test:**

game	*house*	*does*	*another*	*warm*
time	*riding*	*lake*	*front*	*driver*

8. **Sentence dictation:**
All name and titles begin with a capital letter.
- What do all names and titles begin with? **(A capital letter)**

One of these four sentences should have a comma. See if you can get it in the right place!
(Suggestion: Keep a record of individual or team efforts for a special prize.)

1. *I told King Roy to go around to the front of the house.*
2. *The driver tossed the boxes on the ground.*
3. *Does Beth have time to play another game?*
4. *If it is warm, we can go riding around the lake.*

9. **Word search:**
Read the words before you start.

(Write the day and the date on the white board—be sure to do this every day.)

Copy the day and the date into your workbook.

1. **Key sentence review:**
   Write the following sentences:

   1. *We saw who came over.*
   2. *Many of these girls come from England.*
   3. *Some people are always happy.*

2. **Spelling patterns:**
   You are going to write words spelled with *'ea', 'ou'* and *'ai'*. When I say each word, point to the spelling pattern you will use and then write the word.

seat	*mouth*	*afraid*	*mouse*
count	*tail*	*team*	*plain*
paid	*year*	*sound*	*real*

3. **Word sum dictation:**
   - What is the first morpheme in *worthless*? **(worth)**

   Write *worth* in the first blank in Part 3.
   - What is the next morpheme in *worthless*? **(less)**

   Write *less* in the next blank.
   Now write *worthless* in the third blank.
   (Repeat for the following words:)

heat + ed = heated	*loud + est = loudest*
to + night = tonight	*size + able = sizable*
bed + room = bedroom	*mother + ly = motherly*
un + load + ed = unloaded	

3. Continued:

Now cover your work and write these words from dictation.

worthless	*heated*	*loudest*	*tonight*
sizable	*bedroom*	*motherly*	*unloaded*

4. Copying the letters in words:

I'll spell some words and you write them down.
Then tell me what words I spelled.

nothing	*should*	*better*
growl	*wrong*	*reach*

Now cover your work and write these words again on the lines below. *(Dictate the words.)*

5. Word search:

Read the words before you start.

6. Spelling test:

when	*again*	*store*	*why*	*could*
real	*what*	*word*	*many*	*done*
saw	*mind*	*were*	*super*	*twice*
was	*page*	*left*	*want*	*said*
blue	*warm*	*soap*	*who*	*danger*

7. Word sums: *(Optional)*

Make at least eight real words from the following morphemes.
(Teacher may suggest words if necessary.)

un- *load* *dress* *pack* *-ing* *-ed* *-s*

Placement / Mastery Test:

Test to be used after Level 40:

(See the instructions for Mastery Tests on page 6.)

mouse	*coldest*	*hoping*	*homeless*	*which*
gamely	*enjoy*	*driving*	*worrying*	*blue*
round	*rider*	*junk*	*nicely*	*plainly*
warmer	*pencil*	*placed*	*unloaded*	*taking*

Scoring:

Mastery:	*0-3 errors—*	*pass*
	4-7 errors—	*review spelling patterns and retest the following day*
	8+ errors—	*go back to Level 31.*
Placement:	*0-2 errors—*	*pass; start at this level, or go on to the next placement test*
	2+ errors—	*start at Level 31, or go back to the placement test at the end of Level 30*

(At the beginning of each lesson, write the day and date on the white board. For instance, write ***Wednesday, 5 January 2011****.*[*]*)*

At the beginning of each lesson, you will copy the day and date into your workbook. Write the day and the date in your workbook.

1. **Contractions:**

   In Part 1 you are going to match these contractions to their meanings.

he's—he is	*what's—what is*	*there's—there is*
let's—let us	*it's—it is*	*she's—she is*

2. **Substituting contractions:**

   Rewrite the sentences in Part 2 using the contractions above:

   1. ***Let's*** *see why* ***he's*** *jumping up and down.*
   2. ***It's*** *time to see* ***what's*** *going on over there.*
   3. ***There's*** *a good game on today.*
   4. ***She's*** *just in time to go out riding.*

   Now cover the sentences and write them from dictation.
   (Dictate the sentences.)

3. **Writing contractions:**

   Write these contractions from dictation in Part 3:

don't	*let's*	*can't*	*there's*
what's	*it's*	*I've*	*he's*

* Make this standard procedure for all written work. This is a simple and virtually fool-proof method of teaching children to spell the days and months. It is also essential training for writing formal letters.

4. **Key sentence:**

   (On the first line the sentence is partially written with one blank for each missing letter The pupil traces the sentence, filling in the blanks as he goes. Make sure he starts with a capital letter and finishes with a full stop. The pupil then copies the sentence onto line 2, check spelling and punctuation. Cover the work and dictate the sentence, if the pupil gets stuck or makes a mistake, show him the original.)

   The sentence should say *'The Queen has two hundred swans in her front garden.'*

   Trace the sentence, filling in the blanks.

   Copy the sentence onto line 2.

   Now cover up the sentence and write it from dictation on line 3.

5. **Sentence dictation:**

   (Try to get the pupil to remember the whole sentence before he starts writing, as this will help to improve his memory. If he can't, dictate it in chunks—avoid dictating one word at a time.)

   All brand names begin with a capital letter.

   - What do all brand names begin with? **(A capital letter)**

   Coke is a brand name.

   - What should *Coke* begin with? **(A capital letter)**

   Write these sentences.

   1. *If you can wait, there's a nice cold can of Coke at home.*
   2. *I can't stand that tune any more.*
   3. *Let's find out why she's afraid of mice.*
   4. *I don't know what's wrong with her rabbits.*

6. **Crossword:**

   (Pupils should read the words in the puzzle before they start. Imposing a time limit prevents the pupil using it to waste time.)

   Read the words before you start.

Level 42:

(Write the day and the date on the white board—be sure to do this every day.)

Copy the day and the date into your workbook.

1. **Key sentence:**
   The sentence should say *'The Queen has two hundred swans in her front garden.'*
   Trace the sentence, filling in the blanks.
   Copy the sentence onto line 2.
   Now cover up the sentence and write it from dictation on line 3.

2. **Spelling patterns:**
   (New spelling patterns are introduced and tricky spellings reviewed in this exercise. Make sure the pupil has copied correctly before covering and dictating. As with the Key Sentence; show him the original if he forgets the spelling.)
   Read the words in Part 2. *(Prompt if necessary.)*
   Copy them onto line 2.
   Now cover your work and write them from dictation on line 3.

catch	*match*	*pitch*
stretch	*switch*	*scotch*

3. **Word sums:**
   (This exercise introduces the morphemic principle in spelling. Pupils learn to spell the building blocks of more complex words and to join them together.)
   Review morphemes *'able', 'un'* and *'ful'*
   Add these morphemes together:

curable	*unhelpful*	*lovable*
unlikely	*hateful*	*unusable*

Read the words you have written.
Now turn the page and write the words from dictation.
(Dictate the words.)

4. Filling in the blanks:

(The worksheet has a blank for each missing letter. Dictate each word and make sure the pupil traces the word and fills in each blank correctly as he goes.)

Trace the words, filling in the blanks.

warm	*destroy*	*danger*
mouth	*jungle*	*does*

5. Morpheme analysis:

*(The reciprocal of **Word Sums**. Pupils learn to identify the morphemes in words and to separate them.)*

Fill in the blanks to show the morphemes in each word.

with + out	*un + til*	*some + thing*
my + self	*in + to*	*to + day*

6. Writing words:

*(This exercise recycles the words practised in **Filling in the Blanks**. This time the pupil writes the words from dictation.)*

warm	*destroy*	*danger*
mouth	*jungle*	*does*

7. Spelling test:

(Dictate each word. If the pupil is confused by homophones such as be/bee, put the word in context.)

enjoy	*does*	*home*	*there's*	*know*
stretch	*find*	*ghost*	*time*	*game*

8. Sentence dictation:

*(The **Spelling Test** and **Sentence Dictation** should always be done at one sitting, if at all possible, as the spelling test rehearses words used in the dictation, which may be forgotten by the next day.)*

Some of these sentences may have a comma, or maybe none of them do. See if you can get it right!

(Suggestion: Keep a record of individual or team efforts for a special prize.)

1. *Our lovable ghost can't find his way home.*
2. *Does your little sister know how to catch the ball?*
3. *There's not much time left until the game starts, so please be quick.*
4. *She's going to stretch out and enjoy the sun.*

9. Word bingo:

(See page 10 for instructions.)

pencil	*nice*	*other*	*who*
I've	*price*	*when*	*nothing*
said	*what*	*they*	*teacher*
green	*why*	*about*	*black*

(Write the day and the date on the white board—be sure to do this every day.)
Copy the day and the date into your workbook.

1. **New word introduction:**
(Write these words on a white board.)

ready head heavy war water already

Read each word and then spell it out loud.
(Prompt if necessary—then erase the words.)

Now spell the words out loud again.
(Dictate each word and write it on the board as the pupil(s) spell it, correcting errors—then erase the words.)

Now write the words in Part 1.
(Dictate the words in a different order.)

2. **Morpheme analysis:**
Read the words in Part 2.
Fill in the blanks to show the morphemes in each word.

mine + ing	*cure + ed*	*size + able*
leave + ing	*heat + er*	*cloud + less*

Now cover your work and write these words.

mining	*cured*	*sizable*
leaving	*heater*	*cloudless*

3. **Sentence dictation using new words:**
Now you will write some sentences using the words you learned in Part 1.

1. *I hope she's ready to jump into the cold water.*
2. *The big girl has switched on the heater already.*
3. *That marble table is really heavy.*

4. **Key sentence:**
   The sentence should say *'The Queen has two hundred swans in her front garden.'*
   Trace the sentence, filling in the blanks.
   Copy the sentence onto line 2.
   Now cover up the sentence and write it from dictation on line 3.

5. **Copying the letters in words:**
   I'll spell some words and you write them down.
   Then tell me what words I spelled.

pitch	*warm*	*lake*
stir	*behind*	*again*

Now cover your work and write these words again on the lines below. *(Dictate the words.)*

6. **Spelling patterns:**
   You are going to write words spelled with *'ou'*, *'tch'* and *'old'*. When I say each word, point to the spelling pattern you will use and then write the word.

old	*found*	*scotch*
fold	*house*	*matching*

Now write these sentences.

1. *I don't have any matching socks left.*
2. *Your father found some old scotch at our house.*
3. *You should fold your shirts when they are still warm.*

(Write the day and the date on the white board—be sure to do this every day.)

Copy the day and the date into your workbook.

1. **Key sentence review:**
   Write the following sentences:

   1. *Would you make some tea, please?*
   2. *Do you know what my father said?*
   3. *Does she have very many rabbits?*

2. **Spelling patterns:**
   You are going to write words spelled with *'ir'*, *'ice'* and *'ore'*. When I say each word, point to the spelling pattern you will use and then write the word.

stir	*store*	*slice*	*wore*
more	*twice*	*shirt*	*rice*
nice	*bird*	*tore*	*first*

3. **Word sum dictation:**
   - What is the first morpheme in *hoping*? **(hope)**

   Write *hope* in the first blank in Part 3.
   - What is the next morpheme in *hoping*? **(ing)**

   Write *ing* in the next blank.
   Now write *hoping* in the third blank.
   Remember the rule about dropping the *'e'*
   (Repeat for the following words:)

tune + ful = tuneful

my + self = myself

with + out = without

some + thing = something

tune + ing = tuning

hope + ful = hopeful

game + ly = gamely

3. Continued:

Now cover your work and write these words.

hoping	*tuneful*	*tuning*	*myself*
hopeful	*without*	*something*	*gamely*

4. Copying the letters in words:

I'll spell some words and you write them down.
Then tell me what words I spelled.

water	*pitch*	*heavy*
warn	*pound*	*what's*

Now cover your work and write these words again on the lines below. *(Dictate the words.)*

5. Word search:

Read the words before you start.

6. Spelling test:

fix	*clowns*	*there's*	*saving*	*pencils*
don't	*small*	*away*	*shook*	*nothing*
pink	*never*	*crying*	*shove*	*letter*
quiz	*bright*	*strong*	*seat*	*people*
put	*done*	*team*	*shrink*	*England*

7. Word sums: *(Optional)*

Make at least eight real words from the following morphemes.
(Teacher may suggest words if necessary.)

re- *heat* *mark* *store* *-er* *-able* *-ing*

Sentence dictation:

See page 30 for instructions.

All names and titles begin with a capital letter.

- What do all names and titles begin with? **(A capital letter)**

All place names begin with a capital letter.

- What do all place names begin with? **(A capital letter)**

Bonus points for spotting the commas!

1. *You will have to wait until six to catch the bus to Wood Green.*
2. *What's got into the Queen today?*
3. *Were you warned about the danger?*
4. *If you light a match, Tim can find his torch.*
5. *Miss Black can't go without water for much longer.*
6. *Lord North has already switched on the blue light.*
7. *The girl hit me on the head with something heavy.*
8. *There's the boy who left his little brother behind.*
9. *I hate riding home when it is dark.*
10. *Don't you know what time it is?*
11. *The water in our lake is very warm in summer.*
12. *That silver cost the King almost two hundred pounds.*

Apples and Pears Level 46:

(Write the day and the date on the white board—be sure to do this every day.)

Copy the day and the date into your workbook.

1. **Key sentence:**

   The sentence should say *'My uncle got angry because we spent his change.'*
   Trace the sentence, filling in the blanks.
   Copy the sentence onto line 2.
   Now cover up the sentence and write it from dictation on line 3.

2. **Silent *'e'*:**

   You are going to write some words that end with the letter *'e'*.
   - What letter will these words end with? **('e')**

   Listen to each word and you will hear a letter name.

   The first word is *take*.
   - What letter name do you hear in *take*? **(A)**

   Now write *take*.

   The next word is *made*.
   - What letter name do you hear in *made*? **(A)**

   Write *made*.
   *(Repeat this procedure for the following words: *Write these words on the board.)*

same	**white*	*fire*	*hide*	*life*
joke	**whole*	*note*	*pure*	*sure*

3. **Word sum dictation:**

   - What is the first morpheme in *mistaken*? **(mis)**

   Write *mis* in the first blank in Part 3.
   - What is the next morpheme in *mistaken*? **(take)**

   Write *take* in the next blank.
   - What is the next morpheme in *mistaken*? **(en)**

   Write *en* in the next blank.
   Now write *mistaken* in the last blank.
   Remember the rule about dropping the *'e'*

3. Continued:

(Repeat for the following words:)

life + less = lifeless

joke + er = joker

mis + fire + ed = misfired

note + able = notable

un + sure = unsure

un + made = unmade

white + est = whitest

pure + ly = purely

hide + ing = hiding

Now cover your work and spell these words aloud.

(Write the words on the board as the pupil(s) spell them, correcting errors.)

unmade	*whiter*	*firing*	*joked*	*surely*
purest	*taking*	*lifeless*	*hiding*	*notable*

4. Writing words:

Write these silent *'e'* words:

mining	*sizes*	*tuner*	*hopeful*	*cured*
gamely	*ridable*	*nicely*	*timeless*	*placed*

5. Sentence dictation:

Some of these sentences may have a comma, or maybe none of them do. See if you can get it right!

1. *You made that dress two sizes too big for Miss Smith.*
2. *Surely, that must be a mistake.*
3. *I'm sure those pills cured my cold.*
4. *My rifle misfired when I fell into the trench.*

Apples and Pears Level 47:

(Write the day and the date on the white board—be sure to do this every day.)

Copy the day and the date into your workbook.

1. **Key sentence:**
   The sentence should say *'My uncle got angry because we spent his change.'*
   Trace the sentence, filling in the blanks.
   Copy the sentence onto line 2.
   Now cover up the sentence and write it from dictation on line 3.

2. **Spelling patterns:**
   Read the words in Part 2. *(Prompt if necessary.)*
   Copy them onto line 2.
   Now cover your work and write them from dictation on line 3.

off	*stiff*	*stuff*
bread	*dead*	*read*

3. **Word sums:**
   New morpheme *'ness'*
   Add these morphemes together:

illness	*darkness*	*goodness*
kindness	*likeness*	*weakness*

   Read the words you have written.
   Now cover your work and write the words from dictation.

4. **Filling in the blanks:**
   Trace the words, filling in the blanks.

whole	*dinner*	*front*
world	*sure*	*joke*

5. Morpheme analysis:
Fill in the blanks to show the morphemes in each word.

any + thing	*mis + take*	*how + ever*
foot + ball	*my + self*	*mouse + trap + s*

6. Writing words:

whole	*dinner*	*front*
world	*sure*	*joke*

7. Spelling test:

better	*thank*	*she's*	*wants*	*can't*
time	*about*	*made*	*world*	*whole*

8. Sentence dictation:
Some of these sentences may have a comma, or maybe none of them do. See if you can get it right!

1. *She's made a mistake about the time for dinner.*
2. *The whole world wants a better mousetrap.*
3. *Thank goodness they can't find our stuff.*
4. *I've read about the football match already.*

9. Word bingo:
(See page 10 for instructions.)

gang	*soap*	*happy*	*people*
jungle	*ladder*	*slice*	*worry*
felt	*owl*	*hanging*	*really*
walk	*girl*	*good*	*light*

Level 48:

(Write the day and the date on the white board—be sure to do this every day.)

Copy the day and the date into your workbook.

1. **New word introduction:**

   (Write these words on a white board.)

   kettle simple castle apple circle gentle

   Read each word and then spell it out loud.

   (Prompt if necessary—then erase the words.)

   Now spell the words out loud again.

   (Dictate each word and write it on the board as the pupil(s) spell it, correcting errors—then erase the words.)

   Now write the words in Part 1.

   (Dictate the words in a different order.)

2. **Morpheme analysis:**

   Read the words in Part 2.

   Fill in the blanks to show the morphemes in each word.

life + less	*white + est*	*some + thing*
weak + ness	*fire + ing*	*note + able*

   Now cover your work and write these words from dictation.

lifeless	*whitest*	*something*
weakness	*firing*	*notable*

3. **Sentence dictation using new words:**

   Now you will write some sentences using the words you learned in Part 1.

   1. *It's simple to make a castle out of sand.*
   2. *Mother put on the kettle and gave us all apples.*
   3. *Please make a circle with the blue pencil.*

4. Key sentence:

The sentence should say *'My uncle got angry because we spent his change.'*
Trace the sentence, filling in the blanks.
Copy the sentence onto line 2.
Now cover up the sentence and write it from dictation on line 3.

5. Copying the letters in words:

I'll spell some words and you write them down.
Then tell me what words I spelled.

paid	*small*	*blue*
lake	*bread*	*stiff*

Now cover your work and write these words again on the lines below. *(Dictate the words.)*

6. Spelling patterns:

You are going to write words spelled with *'oa', 'ore'* and *'ss'*. When I say each word, point to the spelling pattern you will use and then write the word.

loaf	*shore*	*dress*
wore	*boat*	*classes*

Now write these sentences.

1. *Who paid for the small loaf of bread?*
2. *She wore her blue dress to all of her classes.*
3. *We ran our old boat onto the shore of our lake.*

(Write the day and the date on the white board—be sure to do this every day.)

Copy the day and the date into your workbook.

1. **Key sentence review:**
   Write the following sentences:

   1. *My uncle got angry because we spent his change.*
   2. *The Queen has two hundred swans in her front garden.*
   3. *Does she have very many rabbits?*

2. **Spelling patterns:**
   You are going to write words spelled with *'tch',* *'wor'* and *'age'*. When I say each word, point to the spelling pattern you will use and then write the word.

stretch	*worth*	*cage*	*worry*
word	*page*	*stitch*	*wage*
rage	*scotch*	*worm*	*hatch*

3. **Word sum dictation:**
   - What is the first morpheme in *warned*? **(warn)**

   Write *warn* in the first blank in Part 3.
   - What is the next morpheme in *warned*? **(ed)**

   Write *ed* in the next blank.
   Now write *warned* in the third blank.
   Remember the rule about dropping the *'e'*
   (Repeat for the following words:)

how + ever = however	*kind + ness = kindness*
white + er = whiter	*any + thing = anything*
joke + er = joker	*hide + ing = hiding*
price + less = priceless	

3. Continued:
Now turn the page and write these words from dictation.

warned	*however*	*kindness*	*whiter*
anything	*joker*	*hiding*	*priceless*

4. Copying the letters in words:
I'll spell some words and you write them down.
Then tell me what words I spelled.

heavy	*white*	*does*
circle	*water*	*gentle*

Now cover your work and write these words again on the lines below.
(Dictate the words.)

5. Crossword:
Read the words before you start.

6. Spelling test:

soap	*drift*	*scam*	*walk*	*ladder*
sore	*belt*	*drank*	*cattle*	*rubber*
trip	*again*	*worst*	*table*	*choose*
done	*never*	*other*	*many*	*nothing*
skill	*very*	*don't*	*what's*	*summer*

7. Word sums: *(Optional)*
Make at least eight real words from the following morphemes.
(Teacher may suggest words if necessary.)

re- *mis-* *cord* *take* *form* *-less* *-en* *-er*

Placement / Mastery Test:

Test to be used after Level 49:

(See the instructions for Mastery Tests on page 6.)

hundred	*jumper*	*catches*	*water*	*I've*
joker	*uncle*	*front*	*hiding*	*sure*
pounded	*kettle*	*notable*	*head*	*simple*
lifeless	*swan*	*can't*	*likeness*	*switch*

Scoring:

Mastery: *0-3 errors— pass*
4-7 errors— review spelling patterns and retest the following day
8+ errors— go back to Level 41.

Placement: *0-2 errors— pass; start at this level, or go on to the next placement test*
2+ errors— start at Level 41, or go back to the placement test at the end of Level 40

(At the beginning of each lesson, write the day and date on the white board. For instance, write ***Wednesday, 5 January 2011****.*[*]*)*

At the beginning of each lesson, you will copy the day and date into your workbook. Write the day and the date in your workbook.

1. **The Doubling Rule:**

   When you add a morpheme to a word, sometimes you have to double the final consonant.

   Look at Part 1 in your workbook.

   - How many *M*'s are there in *swim*? **(One)**

   (Say the letter name of M)

   - How many *M*'s are there in *swimming*? **(Two)**
   - How many *D*'s are there in *shred*? **(One)**
   - How many *D*'s are there in *shredding*? **(Two)**

2. **Doubling Words:**

   This is the rule about Doubling Words:

   Doubling Words have only one vowel.

   - How many vowels do Doubling Words have? **(One)**

   That vowel must be second from the end.

   - Where is the vowel in a Doubling Word? **(Second from the end)**

   (Repeat until letter perfect.)

   Find Part 2 on your worksheet. Circle every vowel in each word.

   - How many vowels are there in *lost*? **(One)**
   - Is the vowel second from the end. **(No)**
   - So is *lost* a Doubling Word? **(No)**

   Cross out *lost*.

   - How many vowels are there in *strip*? **(One)**
   - Is the vowel second from the end. **(Yes)**
   - So is *strip* a Doubling Word? **(Yes)**

   Circle the word *strip*.

---

* Make this standard procedure for all written work. This is a simple and virtually fool-proof method of teaching children to spell the days and months. It is also essential training for writing formal letters.

2. Continued:

- How many vowels are there in *broom*? **(Two)**
- So is *broom* a Doubling Word? **(No)**

Cross out *broom*.

- How many vowels are there in *never*? **(Two)**
- So is *never* a Doubling Word? **(No)**

Cross out *never*.

- How many vowels are there in *sad*? **(One)**
- Is the vowel second from the end. **(Yes)**
- So is *sad* a Doubling Word? **(Yes)**

Circle the word *sad*.

3. Doubling Words—practice.

Look at Part 3 on your worksheet.
Circle every vowel in each word.
Circle all the Doubling Words and cross out all the rest.
(If pupils are making mistakes, go back and use the drill in Part 2.)

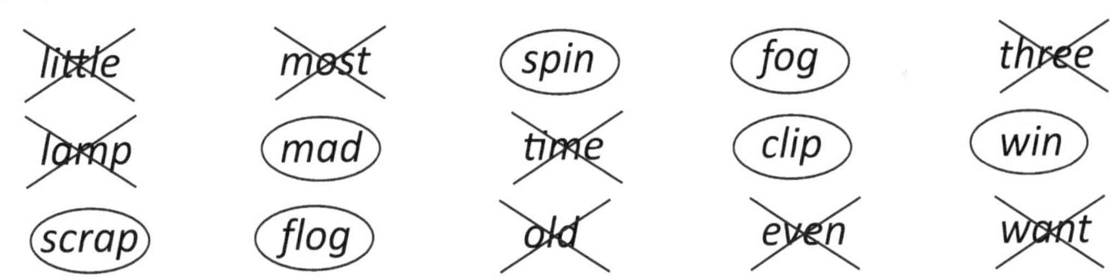

(Write the day and the date on the white board—be sure to do this every day.)
Copy the day and the date into your workbook.

1. **Contractions:**
   In Part 1 you are going to match these contractions to their meanings.

didn't—did not	*what's—what is*	*wasn't—was not*
it's—it is	*isn't—is not*	*aren't—are not*

2. **Substituting contractions:**
   Rewrite the sentences in Part 2 using the above contractions:

   1. *They **aren't** in time for the match today.*
   2. *He **didn't** know **what's** going on.*
   3. *Father **isn't** sure if **it's** time to change.*
   4. *My uncle **isn't** very happy with my rabbit.*

   Now cover the sentences and write them from dictation.

3. **Writing contractions:**
   Write these contractions from dictation:

there's	*don't*	*let's*	*I've*
she's	*what's*	*can't*	*didn't*

4. **Key sentence:**
   The sentence should say *'Can you spare enough money to hire their donkey?'*
   Trace the sentence, filling in the blanks.
   Copy the sentence onto line 2.
   Now cover up the sentence and write it from dictation on line 3.

5. Sentence dictation:

All brand names begin with a capital letter.

- What do all brand names begin with? **(A capital letter)**

Mars is a brand name.

- What should *Mars* begin with? **(A capital letter)**

1. *I wasn't sure why she was hiding my Mars bar.*
2. *There isn't anything left to eat in the house.*
3. *These people aren't likely to buy our swans.*
4. *I don't know what's making Mother so angry.*

Some of these sentences may have a comma, or maybe none of them do. See if you can get it right!

(Suggestion: Keep a record of individual or team efforts for a special prize.)

6. Doubling Words—practice.

Look at Part 3 on your worksheet.

Circle every vowel in each word.

Circle all the Doubling Words and cross out all the rest.

(If pupils are making mistakes, go back and use the drill in 50, Part 2.)

~~clamp~~	~~ford~~	(bag)	~~list~~
(brag)	(strap)	(slip)	(man)
~~brave~~	~~meat~~	(flag)	~~art~~
(big)	~~match~~	~~arch~~	~~tea~~

(Write the day and the date on the white board—be sure to do this every day.)

Copy the day and the date into your workbook.

1. **Key sentence:**

   The sentence should say *'Can you spare enough money to hire their donkey?'*

   Trace the sentence, filling in the blanks.

   Copy the sentence onto line 2.

   Now cover up the sentence and write it from dictation on line 3.

2. **Doubling Words:**

   This is the rule about Doubling Words:

   Doubling Words have only one vowel.

   - How many vowels do Doubling Words have? **(One)**

   That vowel must be second from the end.

   - Where is the vowel in a Doubling Word? **(Second from the end)**

   (Repeat until letter perfect.)

   Circle the Doubling Words in Part 2.

clamp	*train*	*crisp*
(scrap)	*(win)*	*does*

3. **The Doubling rule:**

   This is how you tell when to double the final consonant in a Doubling Word:

   You double the last consonant in a Doubling Word when the next morpheme begins with a vowel.

   Look at Part 3 on your worksheet.

   The first example is *swim + ing*.

   - Is *swim* a Doubling Word? **(Yes)** Circle it.
   - Does *ing* begin with a vowel? **(Yes)** Circle it.
   - Do we double the final *M* in *swimming*? **(Yes)**
   - Spell *swimming* aloud. **(s-w-i-m-m-i-n-g)**

   Write *swimming* on your worksheet.

3. Continued:

The second example is *mad + ly*.

- Is *mad* a Doubling Word? **(Yes)** Circle it.
- Does *ly* begin with a vowel? **(No)**
- Do we double the final *D* in *madly*? **(No)**
- Spell *madly* aloud. **(m-a-d-l-y)**

Write *madly* on your worksheet.

The third example is *help + ing*.

- Is *help* a Doubling Word? **(No)**
- Do we double the final *P* in *helping*? **(No)**
- Spell *helping* aloud. **(h-e-l-p-i-n-g)**

Write *helping* on your worksheet.

The fourth example is *shop + er*.

- Is *shop* a Doubling Word? **(Yes)** Circle it.
- Does *er* begin with a vowel? **(Yes)** Circle it.
- Do we double the final *P* in *shopper*? **(Yes)**
- Spell *shopper* aloud. **(s-h-o-p-p-e-r)**

Write *shopper* on your worksheet.

4. Doubling exercises:

Look at the word-sums in Part 4.
Circle each Doubling Word.
Then look at the second morpheme and circle each one that begins with a vowel.
If both morphemes are circled, you must double the final consonant when you add the morphemes together.

*spi**nn**ing*	*farmer*	*chomping*	*spotless,*
*scra**pp**ed*	*harmful*	*sporting*	*fla**tt**est,*
gladly	*thicken*	*cla**pp**ing*	*sto**pp**able*

5. Crossword:

Read the words before you start.

Level 53:

(Write the day and the date on the white board—be sure to do this every day.)

Copy the day and the date into your workbook.

1. **Key sentence:**
   The sentence should say *'Can you spare enough money to hire their donkey?'*
   Trace the sentence, filling in the blanks.
   Copy the sentence onto line 2.
   Now cover up the sentence and write it from dictation on line 3.

2. **Spelling patterns:**
   Read the words in Part 2. *(Prompt if necessary.)*
   Copy them onto line 2.
   Now cover your work and write them from dictation on line 3.

blue	*true*	*glue*
argue	*third*	*thirsty*

3. **Word sums:**
   New morpheme *'al'*.
   Add these morphemes together:

almost	*already*	*also*
always	*although*	*altogether*

   Read the words you have written.
   Now turn the page and write the words from dictation.

4. **Filling in the blanks:**
   Trace the words, filling in the blanks.

gentle	*sure*	*bread*
circle	*castle*	*whole*

5. **The Doubling Rule:**
   - When do you double the last letter in a Doubling Word?
     (When the next morpheme begins with a vowel.)

   (Repeat until letter perfect.)

   Look at Part 5 on your worksheet.
   The first example is *hot + est*.
   - Is *hot* a doubling word? **(Yes)** Circle it.
   - Does *est* begin with a vowel? **(Yes)** Circle it.
   - Do we double the *T* in *hottest*? **(Yes)**
   - Spell *hottest* aloud. **(h-o-t-t-e-s-t)**

   Write *hottest* on your worksheet.

   The second example is *heat + er*
   - Is *heat* a Doubling Word? **(No)** Cross it out.
   - Do we double the *T* in *heater*? **(No)**
   - Spell *heater* aloud. **(h-e-a-t-e-r)**

   Write *heater* on your worksheet.

   The third example is *flat + ly*.
   - Is *flat* a Doubling Word? **(Yes)** Circle it.
   - Does *ly* begin with a vowel? **(No)** Cross it out.
   - Do we double the *T* in *flatly*? **(No)**
   - Spell *flatly* aloud. **(f-l-a-t-l-y)**

   Write *flatly* on your worksheet.

   Do the rest of the word-sums on your own.

feeling	*scra**pp**ed*	*mousetrap*	
purely	*sna**pp**ing*	*fired*	*goodness*

6. **Writing words:**

gentle	*sure*	*bread*
circle	*castle*	*whole*

7. Spelling test:

because	*switch*	*apples*	*simple*	*aren't*
makes	*didn't*	*very*	*uncle*	*many*

8. Sentence dictation:

1. *My uncle makes very simple mousetraps.*
2. *There aren't many apples left for lunch.*
3. *Thank goodness your father didn't switch off the heater.*
4. *You should be very gentle because she's not feeling well.*

9. Crossword:
Read the words before you start.

Apples and Pears Level 54:

(Write the day and the date on the white board—be sure to do this every day.)

Copy the day and the date into your workbook.

1. **New word introduction:**
   (Write these words on a white board.)

   watch wash oil spoil join joint

   Read each word and then spell it out loud.
   (Prompt if necessary—then erase the words.)

   Now spell the words out loud again.
   (Dictate each word and write it on the board as the pupil(s) spell it, correcting errors—then erase the words.)

   Now write the words in Part 1.
   (Dictate the words in a different order.)

2. Morpheme analysis:
   Read the words in Part 2.
   Fill in the blanks to show the morphemes in each word.

Sun + day	*in + side*	*kind + ness*
glue + ed	*circle + ed*	*al + together*

   Now cover your work and write these words from dictation.

Sunday	*inside*	*kindness*
glued	*circled*	*altogether*

3. **Sentence dictation using new words:**
   Now you will write some sentences using the words you learned in Part 1.

   1. *Wash that oil off your watch or you will spoil it.*
   2. *We always have a joint of pork on Sunday.*
   3. *It's time you joined us inside the circle.*

4. Key sentence:

The sentence should say *'Can you spare enough money to hire their donkey?'*
Trace the sentence, filling in the blanks.
Copy the sentence onto line 2.
Now cover up the sentence and write it from dictation on line 3.

5. Copying the letters in words:

I'll spell some words and you write them down.
Then tell me what words I spelled.

butter	*argue*	*ready*
thirsty	*circle*	*although*

Now cover your work and write these words again on the lines below. *(Dictate the words.)*

6. Spelling patterns:

You are going to write words spelled with *'-mp'*, *'-le'* and *'ea'*. When I say each word, point to the spelling pattern you will use and then write the word.

castle	*bread*	*apple*
lump	*heavy*	*camping*

Now write these sentences.

1. *Are you ready to go camping up by the castle?*
2. *Do you want bread and butter with your apple?*
3. *Let's dump this heavy lump inside the circle.*

7. **The Doubling Rule:**
   - When do you double the last letter in a Doubling Word? **(When the next morpheme begins with a vowel.)**

   (Repeat until letter perfect.)

   Look at Part 7 on your worksheet.

   The first example is *grab + ed*.
   - Is *grab* a Doubling Word? **(Yes)** Circle it.
   - Does *ed* begin with a vowel? **(Yes)** Circle it.
   - Do we double the *B* in *grabbed*? **(Yes)**
   - Spell *grabbed* aloud. **(g-r-a-b-b-e-d)**

   Write *grabbed* on your worksheet.

   The second example is *join + ing*.
   - Is *join* a Doubling Word? **(No)**
   - Do we double the *N* in *joining*? **(No)**
   - Spell *joining* aloud. **(j-o-i-n-i-n-g)**

   Write *joining* on your worksheet.

   The third example is *hat + less*.
   Is *hat* a Doubling Word? **(Yes)** Circle it.
   Does *less* begin with a vowel? **(No)**
   Do we double the *T* in *hatless*? **(No)**
   Spell *hatless* aloud. **(h-a-t-l-e-s-s)**
   Write *hatless* on your worksheet.

   Do the rest of the word-sums on your own.

*sto**pp**er*	*fla**pp**ing*	*washing*	
jobless	*watching*	*kno**tt**ed*	*worldly*

8. **Word bingo:**

   (See page 10 for instructions.)

many	*always*	*boot*	*mean*
nice	*page*	*were*	*toad*
how	*skin*	*blue*	*town*
more	*trouble*	*know*	*these*

(Write the day and the date on the white board—be sure to do this every day.)
Copy the day and the date into your workbook.

1. **Key sentence review:**
   Write the following sentences:

   1. *I never use blue pencils.*
   2. *Does she have very many rabbits?*
   3. *Can you spare enough money to hire their donkey?*

2. **Spelling patterns:**
   You are going to write words spelled with *'ea'*, *'ir'* and *'ue'*. When I say each word, point to the spelling pattern you will use and then write the word.

each	*bird*	*blue*	*squirm*
firm	*dream*	*least*	*argue*
true	*clue*	*shirt*	*easy*

3. **Homophones:**
   Fill in the blank with the right word.
   (***their*** = it belongs to them; "I rode ***their*** donkey."
   there = in that place; "Sit down over ***there***."
   or ***there*** were, ***there*** are, ***there*** was, ***there*** will be...)

   1. *I like **their** house.*
   2. *When will we get **there**?*
   3. ***There** were six girls at home.*
   4. ***There** was a good reason for that.*
   5. ***Their** rabbits are very soft.*
   6. *I put it down over **there**.*

4. Copying the letters in words:

I'll spell some words and you write them down. Then tell me what words I spelled.

heavy	*white*	*does*
circle	*water*	*gentle*

Now cover your work and write these words again on the lines below. *(Dictate the words.)*

5. The Doubling Rule:

- When do you double the last letter in a Doubling Word? **(When the next morpheme begins with a vowel.)**

(Repeat until letter perfect.)

Look at Part 5 on your worksheet.

The first example is *slip + er*.

- Is *slip* a Doubling Word? **(Yes)** Circle it.
- Does *er* begin with a vowel? **(Yes)** Circle it.
- Do we double the *P* in *slipper*? **(Yes)**
- Spell *slipper* aloud. **(s-l-i-p-p-e-r)**

Write *slipper* on your worksheet.

The second example is *coat + ed.*

- Is *coat* a Doubling Word? **(No)**
- Do we double the *T* in *coated*? **(No)**
- Spell *coated* aloud. **(c-o-a-t-e-d)**

Write *coated* on your worksheet.

The third example is *sad + ness*.

- Is *sad* a Doubling Word? **(Yes)** Circle it.
- Does *ness* begin with a vowel? **(No)**
- Do we double the *D* in *sadness*? **(No)**
- Spell *sadness* aloud. **(s-a-d-n-e-s-s)**

Write *sadness* on your worksheet.

Do the rest of the word-sums on your own.

gladly	*ro**bb**er*	*joiner*	
surely	*stretches*	*changing*	*fitness*

6. Spelling test:

want	*dead*	*life*	*war*	*castle*
scotch	*which*	*warm*	*hundred*	*when*
does	*very*	*were*	*who*	*people*
world	*said*	*watch*	*many*	*trouble*
what	*skip*	*wash*	*shore*	*England*

7. Word sums: *(Optional)*

Make at least eight real words from the following morphemes.
(Teacher may suggest words if necessary.)

un- *kind* *like* *love* *drink* *-able* *-ness*

Apples and Pears Level 56:

(Write the day and the date on the white board—be sure to do this every day.)

Copy the day and the date into your workbook.

Sentence dictation:

See page 30 for instructions.

Bonus points for spotting the commas!

1. *Does your mother have a spare room for their rabbits?*
2. *Who said they should change all of our money?*
3. *Don't worry about taking us kids to school.*
4. *Are you sure the ghost is still hanging around their house?*
5. *If you work hard enough, you will make some money.*
6. *Put your coat over there by the white dresser.*
7. *I drank all of the Coke because I was very thirsty.*
8. *We glued little bits of paper together and made a castle.*
9. *Each girl must take home at least five mice.*
10. *You will spoil that jumper if you put it in the hot wash.*
11. *My older brother is always walking around in circles.*
12. *I never saw the white donkey hiding behind the lamppost.*

(Write the day and the date on the white board—be sure to do this every day.)
Copy the day and the date into your workbook.

1. **Key sentence:**
   The sentence should say *'Where shall we hang my friend's pretty picture?'*
   Trace the sentence, filling in the blanks.
   Copy the sentence onto line 2.
   Now cover up the sentence and write it from dictation on line 3.

2. **Silent *'e'*:**
   You are going to write some words that end with the letter *'e'*.
   - What letter will these words end with? **('e')**

   Listen to each word and you will hear a letter name.
   The first word is *name*.
   - What letter name do you hear in *name*? **(A)**

   Now write *name*.

   The next word is *June*.
   - What letter name do you hear in *June*? **(U)**

   Write *June*. *(Repeat this procedure for the following words:)*

safe	*care*	*ale*	*fine*	*bite*
smile	*quite*	*broke*	*smoke*	*rope*

3. **Word sum dictation:**
   - What is the first morpheme in *safely*? **(safe)**

   Write *safe* in the first blank in Part 3.
   What is the next morpheme in *safely*? **(ly)**
   Write *ly* in the next blank.
   Now write *safely* in the last blank.
   Remember the rule about dropping the *'e'*.

3. Continued:

(Repeat for the following words:)

broke + en = broken

rope + ed = roped

care + ing = caring

smile + ing = smiling

un + safe = unsafe

re + fine + ed = refined

care + less + ness = carelessness

smoke + less = smokeless

un + want + ed = unwanted

Now cover your work and write these words.

refined	*smiling*	*safely*	*broken*
unsafe	*roped*	*smokeless*	*caring*
unwanted	*carelessness*		

4. The Doubling Rule:

- When do you double the last letter in a Doubling Word? **(When the next morpheme begins with a vowel.**)

(Repeat until letter perfect.)

Look at Part 4 on your worksheet.
The first example is *trip + ing.*

- Is *trip* a Doubling Word? **(Yes)** Circle it.
- Does *ing* begin with a vowel? **(Yes)** Circle it.
- Do we double the *P* in *tripping*? **(Yes)**
- Spell *tripping* aloud. **(t-r-i-p-p-i-n-g)**

Write *tripping* on your worksheet.

The second example is *water + ed.*

- Is *water* a Doubling Word? **(No)**
- Do we double the *R* in *watered*? **(No)**
- Spell *watered* aloud. **(w-a-t-e-r-e-d)**

Write *watered* on your worksheet.

4. Continued:

The third example is *thin + ly*.

- Is *thin* a Doubling Word? **(Yes)** Circle it.
- Does *ly* begin with a vowel? **(No)**
- Do we double the *N* in *thinly*? **(No)**
- Spell *thinly* aloud. **(t-h-i-n-l-y)**

Write *thinly* on your worksheet.

Do the rest of the word-sums on your own.

hanging	*stu**nn**ing*	*ski**nn**ed*	
*we**tt**est*	*trimness*	*glasses*	*ho**pp**ing*

5. Writing words:

Write these silent *'e'* words:

fire	*life*	*coke*	*whole* *(all of it)*
pure	*tune*	*white*	*size*
page	*rice*		

6. Sentence dictation:

Some of these sentences may have a comma, or maybe none of them do. See if you can get it right!

(Suggestion: Keep a record of individual or team efforts for a special prize.)

1. *I don't care if you smile.*
2. *We aren't quite broke yet.*
3. *If you are careful, you will be safe.*
4. *Let's have a bite to eat and a glass of ale.*

7. Word search:

Read the words before you start.

Level 58:

(Write the day and the date on the white board—be sure to do this every day.)

Copy the day and the date into your workbook.

1. **Key sentence:**
   The sentence should say *'Where shall we hang my friend's pretty picture?'*
   Trace the sentence, filling in the blanks.
   Copy the sentence onto line 2.
   Now cover up the sentence and write it from dictation on line 3.

2. **Spelling patterns:**
   Read the words in Part 2. *(Prompt if necessary.)*
   Copy them onto line 2.
   Now cover your work and write them from dictation on line 3.

point	*coin*	*foil*
moist	*early*	*earth*

3. **Word sums:**
   New morpheme *'be'.*
   Add these morphemes together:

below	*become*	*belong*
beware	*before*	*behave*

   Read the words you have written.
   Now cover your work and write the words from dictation.

4. **Filling in the blanks:**
   Trace the words, filling in the blanks.

money	*theirs*	*enough*
castle	*easy*	*argue*

5. The Doubling Rule:

- When do you double the last letter in a Doubling Word?
  (When the next morpheme begins with a vowel.)

(Repeat until letter perfect.)

Look at Part 5 on your worksheet.

The first example is *jog + ing.*

- Is *jog* a Doubling Word? **(Yes)** Circle it.
- Does *ing* begin with a vowel? **(Yes)** Circle it.
- Do we double the *G* in *jogging*? *(Yes)*
- Spell *jogging* aloud. **(j-o-g-g-i-n-g)**

Write *jogging* on your worksheet.

The second example is *sweet + est.*

Is *sweet* a Doubling Word? **(No)**

- Do we double the *T* in *sweetest*? **(No)**
- Spell *sweetest* aloud. **(s-w-e-e-t-e-s-t)**

Write *sweetest* on your worksheet.

The third example is *man + ly*.

- Is *man* a Doubling Word? **(Yes)** Circle it.
- Does *ly* begin with a vowel? **(No)**
- Do we double the *N* in *manly*? **(No)**
- Spell *manly* aloud. **(m-a-n-l-y)**

Write *manly* on your worksheet.

Do the rest of the word-sums on your own.

really	*smiling*	*gladly*	
fitful	*ge**tt**ing*	*hopeless*	*hi**dd**en*

6. Writing words:

money	*theirs*	*enough*
castle	*easy*	*argue*

7. Spelling test:

easy	*ale*	*isn't*	*wrong*	*care*
take	*fine*	*it's* *(it is)*	*never*	*fire*

8. Sentence dictation:

Some of these sentences may have a comma, or maybe none of them do. See if you can get it right!

1. *Would you care for a glass of our fine ale?*
2. *It's wrong to take all of their money.*
3. *There isn't such a thing as a smokeless fire.*
4. *I would never have dreamed that it would be so easy.*

9. Homophones:

Fill in the blank with the right word.
(***meat*** = something to eat; "I like to eat ***meat***."
meet = get together; "Let's ***meet*** over there.")

1. *Would you like to **meet** their friend?*
2. *We had some cold **meat** for lunch.*
3. *Did you buy any **meat** today?*
4. *When shall we **meet** for lunch?*

Apples and Pears   Level 59:

(Write the day and the date on the white board—be sure to do this every day.)
Copy the day and date into your workbook.

1. **New word introduction:**
   (Write these words on a white board.)

   chance   since   fence   force   notice   office

   Read each word and then spell it out loud.
   (Prompt if necessary—then erase the words.)

   Now spell the words out loud again.
   (Dictate each word and write it on the board as the pupil(s) spell it, correcting errors—then erase the words.)

   Now write the words in Part 1.
   (Dictate the words in a different order.)

2. **Morpheme analysis:**
   Read the words in Part 2.
   Fill in the blanks to show the morphemes in each word.

   un + safe + ly   *de + fine + ing*

   smoke + er   *smile + ing*

   un + sure   *white + est*

   Now cover your work and write these words from dictation.

   unsafely   defining   smoker

   smiling   unsure   whitest

3. **Sentence dictation using new words:**
   Now you will write some sentences using the words you learned in Part 1.

   1. *I've worked for two days since I handed in my notice.*
   2. *Please don't force me to go to the office.*
   3. *Is there any chance of a lift into town?*

4. Key sentence:

The sentence should say *'Where shall we hang my friend's pretty picture?'*
Trace the sentence, filling in the blanks.
Copy the sentence onto line 2.
Now cover up the sentence and write it from dictation on line 3.

5. Copying the letters in words:

I'll spell some words and you write them down.
Then tell me what words I spelled.

spare	*wait*	*donkey*
two	*south*	*hundred*

Now cover your work and write these words again on the lines below. *(Dictate the words.)*

6. Spelling patterns:

You are going to write words spelled with *'ai', 'wa'* and *'ou'*. When I say each word, point to the spelling pattern you will use and then write the word.

train	*bound*	*wash*
again	*watch*	*counted*

Now write these sentences.

1. *I want to watch him wash the dog again.*
2. *You will have a long wait for the south-bound train.*
3. *I counted about two hundred donkeys.*

7. The Doubling Rule:

- When do you double the last letter in a Doubling Word?
  (When the next morpheme begins with a vowel.)

(Repeat until letter perfect.)

Look at Part 7 on your worksheet.
The first example is *in + er.*
- Is *in* a Doubling Word? **(Yes)** Circle it.
- Does *er* begin with a vowel? **(Yes)** Circle it.
- Do we double the *N* in *inner*? **(Yes)**
- Spell *inner* aloud. **(i-n-n-e-r)**

Write *inner* on your worksheet.

The second example is *arm + ed.*
- Is *arm* a Doubling Word? **(No)**
- Do we double the *M* in *armed*? **(No)**
- Spell *armed* aloud. **(a-r-m-e-d)**

Write *armed* on your worksheet.

The third example is *grim + ly.*
- Is *grim* a Doubling Word? **(Yes)** Circle it.
- Does *ly* begin with a vowel? **(No)**
- Do we double the *M* in *grimly*? **(No)**
- Spell *grimly* aloud. **(g-r-i-m-l-y)**

Write *grimly* on your worksheet.

Do the rest of the word-sums on your own.

fencing	*learned*	*kni**tt**ing*	
topless	*bi**gg**er*	*tu**gg**ed*	*shipment*

8. Word search:

Read the words before you start.

Placement / Mastery Test:

Test to be used after Level 59:

(See the instructions for Mastery Tests on page 6.)

glue	*spare*	*washing*	*circle*	*joiner*
argued	*third*	*quite*	*enough*	*June*
pretty	*biting*	*unsafe*	*watched*	*thirsty*
money	*spoiling*	*friend*	*shopping*	*hired*

Scoring:

Mastery: *0-3 errors— pass.*
4-7 errors— review spelling patterns and retest the following day.
8+ errors— go back to Level 50.

Placement: *0-2 errors— pass; start at level 1 in Book C.*
2+ errors— start at Level 50, or go back to the placement test at the end of Level 49.

Apples and Pears A

Apples and Pears A starts by introducing the pupil to correct letter formation and writing single-letter sounds. Children are taught to segment and spell **CVC** words, unambiguous digraphs (e.g.**'ar'** and **'sh'**) are gradually introduced. Common, less predictable spelling patterns, such as **he, she, we** and **my, by, why** are added at a contolled rate. The morphemic principle is introduced in the second half of the book and the correct use of capital letters, full stops and question marks is emphasised throughout. Carefully designed distributed practise and varied exercises ensure that nothing is forgotten.

Apples and Pears C

The use of the apostrophe in possessives is introduced in Apples and Pears C. This level teaches children why we change the **'y'** to **'i'** in **'studies'**, but not in **'studying'**. The emphasis now changes to words of Greek and Latin origin; these are highly predictable in morphology, but they cannot be spelled as they sound. The word **ex-cept-ion-al-ly** consists of 5 building-blocks, all of which can be used in many other words. This reduces the amount that must be memorised to an absolute minimum. It also works in harmony with the 'wordbuilding' exercises in our decoding series, **Dancing Bears** and **Fast Track**, by increasing pupils' awareness of the structure of English words.
Even more importantly, the *meaning* of these words is constantly taught both by definition and in context. The objective is to enable the pupil to feel confident writing academic-level compositions.

Apples and Pears D

We do not recommend that pupils start at this level. However, for older pupils it is very important to carry on with Book D because the number of words the pupil will be able to spell increases enormously. At this stage, the pupil will progress very rapidly. More importantly, the continued use of the morphemic strategy will enable the pupil to remember new spelling much more easily.
This dicatation exercise shows the level of proficiency expected at the end of Apples and Pears D:

- *The author's characters were not believable.*
- *We had a terrible night's sleep on the mountainside.*
- *The captain said that we will resume our voyage as soon as the anchor is up.*
- *It's possible that my father will assist your studies at university.*
- *That chemist's shop normally does very good business.*
- *He reversed the automobile into the garage with great caution.*
- *The planning officials consistently refused to approve the scheme.*